Daily Discoveries for December

Thematic Learning Activities for EVERY DAY

Written by Elizabeth Cole Midgley

Illustrated by Jennette Guymon-King

Additional illustrations by Becky J. Radtke

Teaching & Learning Company

1204 Buchanan St., P.O. Box 10
Carthage, IL 62321-0010

This book belongs to

_____

Several of the activities in this book involve preparing, tasting and sharing food items. We urge you to be aware of any food allergies or restrictions your students may have and to supervise these activities diligently. All food-related suggestions are identified with this allergy-alert symbol: ⚠

Please note: small food items (candies, raisins, cereal, etc.) can also pose a choking hazard.

Cover art by Jennette Guymon-King

Copyright © 2005, Teaching & Learning Company

ISBN No. 1-57310-465-5

Printing No. 987654321

Teaching & Learning Company
1204 Buchanan St., P.O. Box 10
Carthage, IL 62321-0010

The purchase of this book entitles teachers to make copies for use in their individual classrooms, only. This book, or any part of it, may not be reproduced in any form for any other purposes without prior written permission from the Teaching & Learning Company. It is strictly prohibited to reproduce any part of this book for an entire school or school district, or for commercial resale.

All rights reserved. Printed in the United States of America.

At the time of publication every effort was made to insure the accuracy of the information included in this book. However, we cannot guarantee that agencies and organizations mentioned will continue to operate or maintain these current locations.

Table of Contents

December 1	Basketball Day	5
December 2	Alaska National Park Day	15
December 3	Illinois Admission Day	22
December 4	Reindeer Mania Day	29
December 5	Martin Van Buren's Birthday	41
December 6	No More Slavery Day	45
December 7	Winter Weather Day	52
December 8	Evergreen Appreciation Day	58
December 9	Joel Chandler Harris' Birthday	64
December 10	Human Rights Day	69
December 11	Indiana Statehood Day	75
December 12	Poinsettia Day	80
December 13	It's a Small World Day	86
December 14	South Pole Day	94
December 15	Hanukkah Day (varies)	100
December 16	Ludwig Van Beethoven's Birthday	106
December 17	Hands On Day	112
December 18	Nutcracker Day	120
December 19	Gumballs Galore Day	125
December 20	Puzzles and Pieces Day	132
December 21	Crossword Puzzle Day	136
December 22	Cloud Nine Day	140
December 23	Japanese Emperor's Birthday	149
December 24	Christmas Eve Day	153
December 25	Christmas Day	157
December 26	Kwanzaa Day	162
December 27	Quilt-Mania Day	165
December 28	Woodrow Wilson's Birthday	168
December 29	Igloos and Eskimos Day	172
December 30	Rudyard Kipling's Birthday	179
December 31	New Year's Eve Day	183
December Games		188
December Calendar		192

Dear Teacher or Parent,

Due to the stimulus of a high-tech world, parents and teachers are often faced with the challenge of how to capture the attention of a child and create an atmosphere of meaningful learning opportunities. Often we search for new ways to meet this challenge and help young people transfer their knowledge, skills and experiences from one area to another. Subjects taught in isolation can leave a feeling of fragmentation. More and more educators are looking for ways to be able to integrate curriculum so that their students can fully understand how things relate to each other.

The Daily Discoveries series has been developed to that end. The premise behind this series has been, in part, the author's educational philosophy: anything can be taught and absorbed by others in a meaningful way, depending upon its presentation.

In this series, each day has been researched around the history of a specific individual or event and has been developed into a celebration or theme with integrated curriculum areas. In this approach to learning students draw from their own experience and understanding of things, to a level of processing new information and skills.

The Daily Discoveries series is an almanac-of-sorts, 12 books (one for each month) that present a thematically based curriculum for grades K-6. The series contains hundreds and hundreds of resources and ideas that can be a natural springboard to learning. These ideas have been used in the classroom and at home, and are fun as well as educationally sound. The activities have been endorsed by professors, teachers, parents and, best of all, by children.

The Daily Discoveries series can be used in the following ways for school or home:
- to develop new skills and reinforce previous learning
- to create a sense of fun and celebration every day
- as tutoring resources
- as enrichment activities that can be used as time allows
- for family fun activities

Sincerely,

Elizabeth

Elizabeth Cole Midgley

Basketball Day

December 1

Setting the Stage
- Set up a bulletin board display of pictures of famous basketball players. Include pictures of your school's basketball team. Use the caption: "We're on the Ball and Making Points!" Place a stack of paper basketballs next to the board. Let students write on the basketballs goals they have accomplished this school year (making straight A's, reading a certain number of books, learning their multiplication tables, etc.). They can add their basketballs to the board. See the pattern on page 12.

- Construct a semantic web with facts your students already know (or would like to know) about the game of basketball.

Historical Background
On this day in 1891, James Naismith, a physical education teacher in Springfield, Massachusetts, created a sport that could be played indoors in the winter. He attached peach baskets to two sides of the gym and challenged his students to throw soccer balls into them. The game was called basketball. It has become one of the most popular sports in America, and the world!

Literary Exploration
Basketball Buddies by Jean Marzollo
Dikembe Mutombo by Mark Stewart
Friday Nights (The Broadway Ball Players) by Maureen Holohan
Grant Hill by John Rolfe
I Can Be a Basketball Player by Kathy Henderson
Michael Jordan by Phil Berger
Shaquille O'Neal by Edward Tallman
Soup's Hoop by Robert Newton Peck

Language Experience

- Let students explain how to play the game of basketball, including the procedures and rules.

- Divide students into two teams and have them debate the pros and cons of playing basketball. What's good about it? (good exercise, teaches teamwork and cooperation) What's bad about it? (only the best players may get to play, takes a lot of time)

- Challenge students to come up with colorful words to describe basketball (not just *exciting*, but *hair-raising, heart-stirring*). List the words on the board. Then have students put them in alphabetical order.

Writing Experience

- Challenge students to write poems about the game of basketball. They can choose one of the following kinds of poems:

Rhyme
At least four lines with the last word in every two lines or every other line rhyming

Acrostic
An unrhymed poem where the first letter in each line spells out the word *basketball*

Haiku
Three unrhymed lines with five syllables in the first and third lines and seven syllables in the second line

Cinquain
An unrhymed poem of five lines:
Line 1: one word that names the subject
Line 2: two words that describe the subject
Line 3: three "ing" verbs that describe actions related to the subject
Line 4: four words that express a feeling about the subject
Line 5: one word that describes or renames the subject

Write instructions for the different kinds of poems on the board for students to see as they write.

Writing Experience continued

- Add a little whimsy to the day by having students imagine that they are basketballs. Have them write their feelings during a big game. Is the basketball angry at being bounced and thrown around, excited to be a part of the game, scared about being treated so roughly? When all the papers are completed, let volunteers read theirs aloud with feeling. Students can write their ideas on the pattern on page 13.

- Divide students into small groups. Have them work together to write puppet skits involving basketball players. The characters may be friends or famous professional athletes such as Michael Jordan, Magic Johnson, etc. The skit may be of a basketball game in progress, a discussion between players, a TV interview or whatever the group wants to do. Allow time for them to write the script and practice it with puppets they have made. See page 10 for directions for making the puppets they will use to act out the skits.

Math Experience

- Read aloud the following basketball math problems for students to solve:

    In the basketball game between South Hill and West View schools, two players scored their personal best for the season. Brian Lane of South Hill scored 18 points. Jake Myers made 23 points. How many more points did Jake score?

    At the basketball tournament, the Kennedy Middle School team beat Central by 11 points. Kennedy's final score was 38. How many points did Central have?

    Chris Mattson is the top scorer for the year on her Junior High basketball team. She beat another player, who scored 97 points, by 7 points. How many points did Chris score?

    Have students share their answers and explain how they solved the problems.

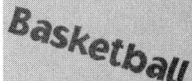

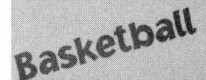

- Challenge each student to write a basketball-related math problem for other students to solve. Then have students exchange problems. Students should solve the problems on another sheet of paper, then exchange problems with someone else. Keep the exchange going until each student has solved five different math problems. Then share answers.

Math Experience

- Have students poll schoolmates to find out which is the more popular sport: basketball, baseball or football. Let them tally their findings and show the results on a class bar graph.

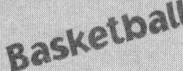

Science/Health Experience

- Let students measure one another's height. When they have a list of everyone's height, show them how to add the numbers together, then divide them by the number of students to get the average height of students in your class. Then challenge them to do some research to find out the height of well-known basketball players such as Michael Jordan, Shaquille O'Neal, Yao Ming, etc. Again, have them list the heights, then divide the total by the number of players to get the average height. Compare the two averages. Ask students why they think most basketball players have to be so tall.

Social Studies Experience

- Let students research to discover interesting biographical facts about famous basketball players such as: Michael Jordan, Shaquille O'Neal, Larry Bird, Charles Barkley, Wilt Chamberlain, Magic Johnson, etc. Let them share the information with the rest of the class.

- Let students go to the internet to find out the names of the professional basketball teams in the United States and where they are from. Compile a list. Then have students point out the towns these teams represent on a United States map. Have a class vote to see which team is the most popular.

Music/Dramatic Experience

- Play some lively music and let students pantomime a basketball game (dribbling the ball, shooting baskets, running, jumping, etc.).

- Play slower music and have students pantomime a basketball player's moves in slow motion.

- Work together to write a class song in praise of basketball to a familiar tune such as "Row, Row, Row Your Boat." Write the words on the board as students suggest them.
    (Example: Basketball is fun.
                We just love to play.
                Running, jumping, scoring points.
                We play it every day.)
  Sing the completed song together. Perform it for other classes.

Physical/Sensory Experience

- Divide students into two teams and let them play a silent game of balloon basketball. Provide a blown-up balloon and a round wastebasket. They'll need to play carefully to keep the balloon from popping. Specify that no dribbling is required in this game and that no talking or yelling by players or audience is allowed. Clear one end of the room for the game. Keep a spare balloon handy in case the first one bursts. The team responsible for bursting the balloon gets a 10-point penalty. Let only five people at a time play on each team. Change the players often so everyone gets a chance to play.

- Bring a basketball to class. Pass it around the room, letting students hold it. Give each student a chance to bounce the basketball and catch it.

- If you have a basketball goal in your playground, take students outside and let each of them have a turn to try to throw a basketball at the basket. Older students may want to divide into two teams and play a short game of basketball while non-participants watch and cheer them on. Some non-participants may want to act as cheerleaders and come up with their own cheers.

Arts/Crafts Experience

- Your students will enjoy working together to create a wall display to honor your school's basketball teams. Assign jobs. You'll need a couple of students to obtain photographs of the teams, a few students to design the layout of the display, students to draw and cut out letters for the caption, students to draw pictures and a few students to actually assemble the display on a wall outside your classroom (or wherever you get permission to put it). Use a simple caption, such as: "Our Basketball Teams Are Tops!" Or you may choose to select a small group of students to come up with a catchy caption for the display. Have the good artists in your class draw pictures of basketball games and cheerleaders leading fans in encouraging cheers. When the display is completed, be sure to invite the rest of the school to come by for a look.

- Let students make moveable basketball player puppets. Have them color body parts and draw features such as hair, eyes, etc., and draw basketball uniforms on the figures on page 14. Then they can connect the arms and legs to the body with brad fasteners so they can be moved into different postures. Have them glue the top of each puppet to a tongue depressor for a handle. Students can use the puppets to act out basketball games, sports interviews, etc. Copy the patterns on page 14 on cardstock for durability. See page 7 for instructions for writing puppet skits.

- Bring a Wheaties™ cereal box to class for students to see (one with a famous athlete on it). Explain that the cereal has for many years featured athletes from various sports (basketball, baseball, football, tennis, track, gymnastics, etc.). Encourage students to design new Wheaties™ box covers featuring their favorite basketball players. These may be well-known professional basketball players or players from the school teams. Display the completed artwork on the classroom wall around the Wheaties™ cereal box.

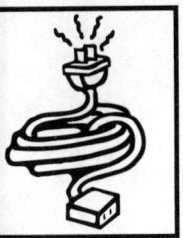

Extension Activities

- Invite the coach of your school's basketball teams to visit your class and talk about basketball. Let your students ask questions.

- Get permission for your class to go to the gym together and watch one of the basketball teams practice. Afterward, let students share what they learned.

Values Education Experience

- Discuss the need for cooperation and teamwork among basketball players. How is the team affected if one player "hogs" the ball and always tries to make baskets rather than practicing teamwork? What happens if one player on the team doesn't want to do what the coach says? Where else is teamwork important?

Follow-Up/Homework Idea

- Encourage students to get their families involved in playing basketball or attending a basketball game at your school together.

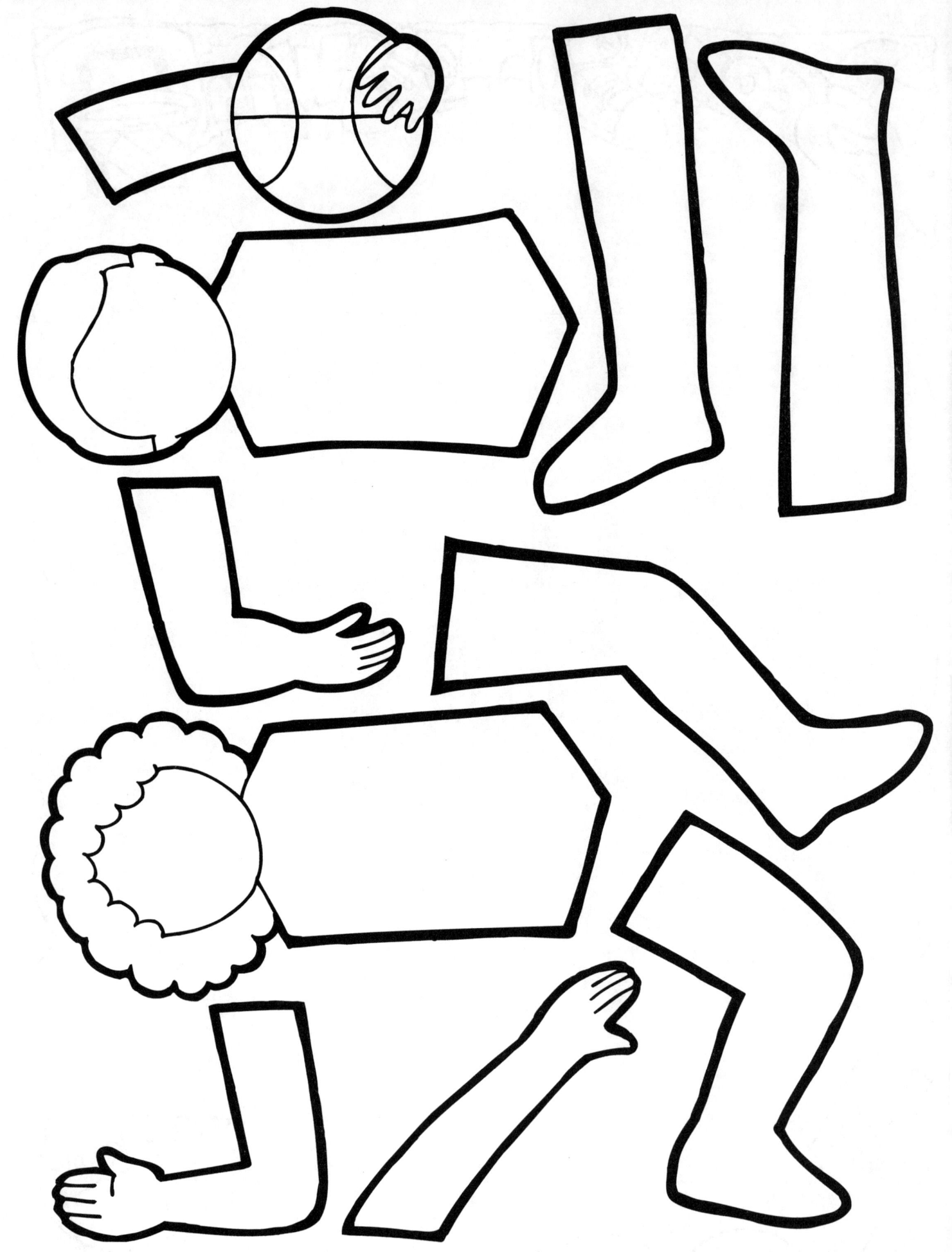

Alaska National Park Day

December 2

Setting the Stage
- Display a map of Alaska on a bulletin board. Stick red map pins in the six spots where the national parks, listed below, are located. Surround the map with pictures of Alaskan wildlife (bears, moose, foxes, mountain goats, etc.) and trees and plants. Look in nature magazines for pictures you can use. At the top of the board place this caption: "Let's Go Wild in Alaska!"

- Construct a semantic web with facts your students already know (or would like to know) about Alaska.

Historical Background
On this day in 1980, six different national parks were established in the state of Alaska—Gates of the Arctic, Glacier Bay, Katami, Kenai Fjords, Kobuk Valley and Lake Clark.

Literary Exploration
Alaska by Dennis B. Fradin
Alaska ABC Book (Last Wilderness Adventure) by Charlene Kreeger
Alaska: "Crinkum-Crankam": A Funny Word Book About Our State by Carole Marsh
Alaska (Rookie Read-About Geography) by Su Tien Wong
Far North in the Arctic: Counting Alaska's Animals by Cory Cooper Hansen, et al.
Frozen Stiff by Sherry Shahan
Julie of the Wolves by Jean Craighead George
My First Book About Alaska by Carole Marsh and Kathy Zimmer
Orcas Around Me: My Alaskan Summer by Deborah Page

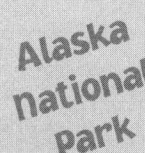

Language Experience

- Have students print the word *ALASKA* vertically on their papers. Challenge them to create an acrostic of words to describe what they might see in Alaska. Each word needs to begin with one of the letters from the word. Here's a rhyming acrostic you can print on the board to inspire them, though their acrostics do not need to rhyme. If some students want to try a rhyming acrostic, let them.

> **A**laska is great;
> **L**ove it, I do!
> **A**lmost like a trip to
> **S**eattle's zoo!
> **K**odiak bears, wolves and moose!
> **A**ll here in Alaska, running around loose!

- Create a class Venn diagram with similarities and differences between Alaska and the state in which you live.

- Have students name animals they might see in Alaska's national parks. They can look through books or magazines about Alaska if they need help. Write them on the board. When the list if done, have them put the animals in alphabetical order.

- Have students count the number of times the vowel "a" is used in the word *Alaska*. What other state names include vowels repeated three times? (Illinois, Arkansas, Colorado, New Jersey, Virginia, West Virginia) Are there any state names that use the same vowel more times? (Alabama, Tennessee) Try the same activity with consonants. (Connecticut—3 Cs, Massachusetts—4 Ss, Mississippi—3 i's and 4 Ss, Pennsylvania—3 Ns)

Writing Experience

- After students have an opportunity to look in magazines and books to see what it's like in Alaska, let them pretend they are on vacation at a park in Alaska. Have them write postcards home, describing what they have seen and done. They can write their message on one side of the card, then draw an Alaskan picture on the other side. Let them exchange postcards so they can share one another's Alaskan adventures.

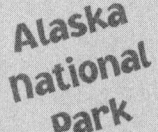

Writing Experience continued

- Let students imagine what it would be like to live in Alaska, The Land of the Midnight Sun. Discuss why it is called that and talk about other unique aspects of Alaska. Have each student write a first-hand account of a year living in the wilds of Alaska. Who is with them? Where do they live? How do they spend their time? What problems do they encounter? Encourage them to use their imaginations, but also be accurate with their facts. (Example: They might run into a moose or bear, but certainly not a tiger!) Have them write their Alaskan Adventures on the pattern on page 21.

- Have students write short stories about Alaska, using these story starters:

    I heard a noise at the cabin door. When I opened it, there stood a baby bear . . .

    As I flew over the mountains, the engine of the plane suddenly began to sputter and miss. I looked around to find a place to land quickly . . .

    As a park ranger, it was my job to try to keep the wild animals and the park visitors from causing problems for one another, but one day . . .

    I hitched up my team of dogs to the sled and off we went, skimming over the icy ground through the cold morning. The other racers were far ahead, but I . . .

Math Experience

- Tell students that the state of Alaska is a place with a diverse population. Write the following numbers on the board as you talk about them:

434,534	white people
98,043	American Indians or Alaska Natives
25,116	Asians
21,787	African Americans
3308	Hawaiians or Pacific Islanders
9997	Other groups

Have students copy the numbers and add them together to find the total population of Alaska. (592,785 (2003 census)) Have them look up the population of your state to see how the numbers compare. Is your state's population larger or smaller than Alaska's? (If you live in Alaska, choose another state with which to compare your population.)

Math Experience continued

- Show students a road map of Alaska. Have them use the mileage scale to figure out how far it is from one place to another:
  from Anchorage to Lake Clark National Park
  from Fairbanks to Denali National Park
  from Fort Greele to the Yukon Wildlife Refuge

Since there aren't a lot of highways in Alaska, ask students how long it would take them to travel these distances in a small plane, flying at 80 miles an hour.

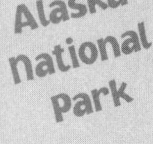

Science/Health Experience

- Have some students research the Northern Lights (Aurora Borealis), then share their findings with the rest of the class.

- The weather in much of Alaska is pleasant in the summer, when most people visit the state. The days are very long, especially around mid-June. The sun may shine for 18-24 hours, which is why it is called The Land of the Midnight Sun. Ask students how they think these warm temperatures and extremely long days would affect vegetable gardens and flowers? (Alaskan gardeners have been known to grow lettuce that weight up to 85 pounds!) Point out that Alaskan winters are just the opposite, extremely cold (20 to 30 below 0) and very little sunlight. Some parts of Alaska above the Arctic Circle experience 24-hour darkness during some winter days. Ask students to discuss what effect the cold and darkness would have on people and plants. Have students compare Alaska's weather with the weather in your state. (If you live in Alaska, choose another state with which to compare your weather.) Ask students what they would enjoy about 18-24 hours of daylight in the summer. What wouldn't they like about it.

- This is a great time to study glaciers, since Alaska has many of them.

Social Studies Experience

- Have students study a map of Alaska and count all the national parks and wildlife refuges they find. Then have them look at maps of other states (Colorado, Utah, Illinois, Texas). How many national parks and wildlife refuges can they find in these other states. Can they see differences between these states and Alaska just by looking at the maps? How is Alaska different? (more wilderness areas, fewer towns and cities, fewer roads)

- Have students research to find out how Alaska's size, in square miles, compares with other states. How does it compare with your state? (If you live in Alaska, choose another state with which to compare your state's size.)

- Encourage interested students to find out all they can about the Iditarod, the annual dogsled race in Alaska. Ask them to share their findings with the rest of the class.

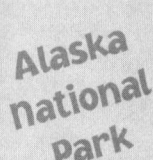

Music/Dramatic Experience

- Have students work in pairs or threes to role-play "How We Spent Our Alaskan Vacation." You may want to spend some time brainstorming activity ideas together before they decide what they want to role-play. Ideas may include: fishing, mountain climbing, hiking, looking for animals, camping, taking pictures, etc. The role plays should include conversation and comments from the students without actually saying what they are doing.

- Challenge students to act like their favorite Alaskan animals, including the sounds they make!

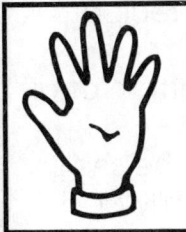

Physical/Sensory Experience

- Divide students into teams and let them compete in dogsled races. Each team chooses one student to be the dogsled "musher" or driver. All the other students are the dogs. They line up in twos. The "dog" pairs hold hands, using their other hands to hook onto the "dogs" in front of them (at the shoulder or waist). The "musher" is at the back, holding onto the "dogs" immediately in front of him or her. Line up the lead "dogs" at the starting line and at your signal the "mushers" yell, "Mush!" to get the team started running toward the goal. Everyone must stay connected and in line. The winning team is the one whose "musher" crosses the finish line first.

Arts/Crafts Experience

- Students always enjoy making snowflakes. Provide them with white paper and scissors and have them follow these simple instructions:

    1. Cut out a circle about 6" in diameter.
    2. Fold the circle in half three times.
    3. Cut designs on the folded edges.
    4. Unfold the circle for the snowflake.
    5. Hang the snowflakes around the room

- Let students use crayons to draw the Northern Lights on art paper. Then have them paint over the picture with black watercolor paint. The colorful scene will resist the paint and make a beautiful picture.

Extension Activities continued

- If there's a national park in your area, invite a park ranger to come to your class to talk to the students about the challenges of protecting the park's natural environment while making it available to visitors. Afterward, talk about the many national parks, such as Yellowstone and Yosemite, in the United States. Ask students who have visited national parks to tell about them. Talk about how these places are a benefit to us.

- Invite someone from the community who has taken a trip to Alaska to visit your class and give a talk and show pictures.

- Make Baked Alaska Tarts as a special treat for students. You may even want to let them help you make them. Try this simple recipe:

  1. Spread 3 tablespoons of currant or grape jelly on the bottom of a tart shell.
  2. Place a scoop of vanilla ice cream on top of the jelly in the shell.
  3. Beat 2 egg whites in a bowl until they are foamy. Gradually add 3 tablespoons of sugar, a dash of salt and $1/4$ teaspoon of vanilla. As you add these ingredients, continue beating the mixture.
  4. Pour the mixture over the ice cream and bake the tart shell at 450°F for about 3 minutes until slightly browned.
  5. Make one tart for each student.
  6. Eat them immediately!

Values Education Experience

- Talk about why patience and adaptability are needed to live in the Alaskan wilderness. How do these character traits help us succeed wherever we live?

Follow-Up/Homework Idea

- Encourage students to ask their parents if they know anyone who lives in Alaska, or if they have been there themselves. Have students share what they learned about Alaska with their families.

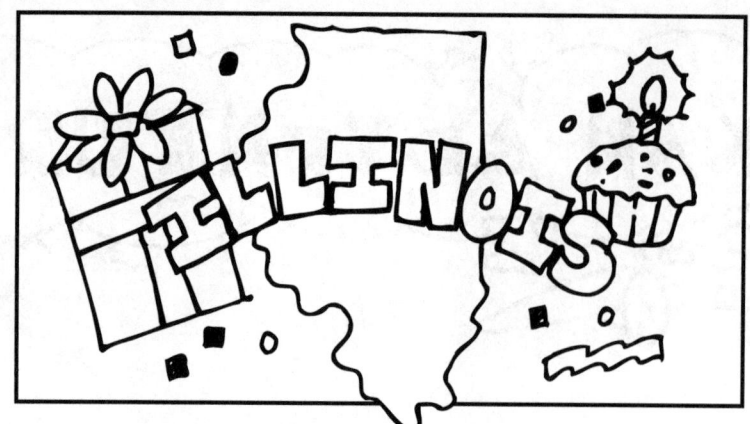

Illinois Admission Day

December 3

Setting the Stage

- Mount a United States map on a bulletin board. Place a big star on the state of Illinois. Gather pictures of Illinois wildlife, scenery and people. Scatter them around the map. Connect the pictures to Illinois on the map with thin ribbon or yarn. Across the top of the board add the caption: "Happy Birthday, Illinois!"

- Construct a semantic map or web with facts your students know (or would like to know) about the state of Illinois. Have them list questions about Illinois they would like to have answered.

- Set up your classroom to represent the state of Illinois today. Put a sign on the door that says Welcome to Illinois! Cut out a large shape of the state from poster board and mount it on a wall. As students discover interesting facts about Illinois today, they can write them on the shape. Divide the room into various areas to represent the different aspects of Illinois. In one area mount pictures of cornfields and farm animals. Place ears of corn and a bale of hay beneath the pictures. In another area, display pictures of Chicago, including Lake Michigan, Navy Pier, Wrigley Field, etc. Continue around the room featuring other aspects of Illinois. Encourage students who have visited or lived in Illinois to bring souvenirs, photos and memorabilia to add to the displays.

Historical Background

On this day in 1818 Illinois became the 21st state in the U.S.A.

Literary Exploration

Across Five Aprils by Irene Hunt
A Long Way from Chicago by Richard Peck
Illinois by Marlene Targ Brill
Illinois by Dennis B. Fradin
L Is for Lincoln: An Illinois Alphabet by Kathy-Jo Wargin
The Story of the Great Chicago Fire by Mary Kay Phelan

Language Experience

- Illinois' name was given to it by French explorers. They named it after the Illiniwek people, Native Americans who lived in the area when the French came there. Teach your students some French words:

bonjour *(bo-zhure)*	good morning
bonsoir *(bo-swah)*	good evening
c'est la vie *(say lah vee)*	that's life
n'est-ce pas? *(nes-pah?)*	isn't it so?
merci *(mare-see)*	thank you
s'il vous plait *(see-vou-play)*	if you please

  Let students roll these words around on their tongues, saying them to each other, as they imagine French explorers discovering the land of Illinois.

- Have students brainstorm words or phrases that rhyme with *Illinois* that could be used as state slogans. (Example: Illinois, what a joy!)

- Play a game of Going to Illinois. Seat students in a big circle. Choose a student to begin, saying: "I'm going to Illinois and I'm going to take an ___." The student must mention something that starts with the first letter of the alphabet, A (apple, atlas, etc.). The next student repeats what the first student said and adds another item, this one beginning with the second letter of the alphabet, B. ("I'm going to Illinois and I'm going to take an apple and a baseball.") Continue around the circle this way. If a student can't remember one of the items, he or she is out of the game. Keep going as long as students can do it.

Writing Experience

- Let students write short stories about the early days in the history of Illinois. They can write about explorers, hunters and trappers, pioneers, farmers or other people who helped to settle the area before the days of the big cities.

- Have students write first-person Illinois adventures, using these story starters:

  The wind began to blow as the sky grew dark and the waves slapped against our small boat on Lake Michigan.

  As I walked down the dusty road, all I could see around me were tall fields of corn. Suddenly, a deer walked out of the corn and stopped right in front of me.

  Mom and I got off the bus in downtown Chicago. We were ready to shop till we dropped. But as soon as the bus rolled off, Mom realized she had left her purse on the seat!

Math Experience

- The population of Illinois as of 2003 was 12,653,544. Write that number on the board. Its population is the fifth largest of all 50 states. More than half of the population live in Chicago and the surrounding area. Challenge students to figure out about how many people that is.

- Illinois' highest point of elevation is 376 meters; its lowest point is 85 meters. Have students figure out the difference. Have them compare these numbers as well as the population number with those of your state.

- Print the alphabet on the board with an amount of money next to each letter. Then write down the names of some of Illinois' cities (Chicago, Springfield, Rockford, Elgin, Carbondale, etc.). Tell students they are going to travel to these cities by train. Their train fare can be figured out by adding the money amounts for the letters in the names of the towns. (Example: If A = $1, C = $3, G = $7, H = $8, I = $9, O = $15, the fare to Chicago would be $46.) Have students work in pairs to figure out how much it will cost them to travel to each city.

Science/Health Experience

- The state bird of Illinois is the cardinal. Have students find out all they can about cardinals, then share their findings with one another. One interesting piece of information is that Illinois school children voted on the state bird in 1928 and the cardinal won! After students share information about cardinals, have them suggest official "class" birds. Vote to see which bird is chosen to represent your class.

- Have students research to find out the average temperatures in winter and summer in Illinois. Remind them that the temperatures in southern Illinois vary considerably from those in the northern part of the state. Compare their findings with the temperatures in your state. (If you live in Illinois, choose another state with which to compare temperatures.)

Social Studies Experience

- Illinois is known as The Land of Lincoln because Abraham Lincoln, our 16th President, grew up there and practiced law in Springfield, the capital city. This would be a good time to study Lincoln, especially his life before he became President.

- Show students a map of the United States. Ask them to list the states they would go through if their family drove to Illinois. Can they figure out about how far away Chicago is from where they live? Ask them to estimate how long the drive would take. What interesting places would they pass along the way? What would they like to stop and see? (If you live in Illinois, suggest that students answer these questions as if they were traveling to Georgia.)

- Illinois is considered part of the Midwest. Ask students to tell the names of other states in the Midwest.

- This is a good time to study the history of the great Chicago fire.

Music/Dramatic Experience

- Corn is a crop that is grown in much of Illinois, not sweet corn that people eat, but field corn which is fed to animals. Ask how many students have seen a field of corn growing in the sun and waving in the breeze. Play some lively music and let students pretend to be cornstalks. They should start out very small, then grow taller and taller. Encourage them to pantomime what it's like to be corn in sun, rain and wind, and even what it's like to be picked.

Physical/Sensory Experience

- Have students play a game of Chicago Fire Tag. Choose two students—one to be the fire and one to be the water hose. The student who is the fire runs around trying to tag other students. When a student is tagged, he or she has to slowly bend over as if melting. They must stay where they are out of the action until the water hose comes by and tags them to put out the fire. To make the game more interesting, blindfold the fire and the water hose! Confine the game to a large circle or portion of the room.

Arts/Crafts Experience

- Let students make Illinois state flags. Have them color the Illinois state seal, page 28, then cut it out and glue it to a white fabric or felt rectangle. They can wrap the left side of the flag around a plastic drinking straw and glue it on for a flagpole. Have them follow these directions for coloring the state seal for accuracy:

    eagle—brown and white with orange beak and feet
    banner—red
    rock—gray
    leaves/garland—dark green
    sun—orange with yellow rays
    shield—red and white stripes, white stars on a dark blue background

  See the pattern on page 28.

- Have students draw pictures of the cardinal, Illinois' state bird. Display some photographs of cardinals for them to look at as they draw.

- Challenge students to design "Welcome to Illinois" billboards, featuring some of the best things about the state. Remind them that billboards use lots of pictures and few words to communicate their message to people driving quickly by. When the designs are done, hang them around the room for everyone to see. You may even want to send them to the governor's office in Illinois!

Extension Activities

- Chicago pizza is a popular treat, not just in Illinois, but wherever people can get it. Bring some to class so your students can have a real treat.

- Let students play an Illinois personalities version of 20 Questions. Write the names of some famous people from Illinois on slips of paper. Put them in a paper bag and let students pull them out. They can answer questions about the person, but only with a "yes" or "no." Make sure the people are ones your students know a lot about (Michael Jordan, Abraham Lincoln, Oprah Winfrey, Jesse Jackson, etc.).

Values Education Experience

- Chicago, Illinois is known as The Windy City. Someone has said that it's called that because the people in Chicago talk a lot! That isn't true, but it brings up a good point to discuss. Ask students when talking is good and when it's not. How can talking too much be a problem? How can talking too little also be a problem? Why is it important to be able to talk clearly and intelligently? Why is it important to know when to speak and when not to speak?

Follow-Up/Homework Idea

- Have students ask their parents if they've ever been to Illinois. If so, what did they like about it? If they have never been there, where in Illinois would they like to go and why?

Reindeer Mania Day

December 4

Setting the Stage

- Come to school with a dab of red lipstick on your nose. Explain that Rudolph, the Reindeer kissed you on the nose. (Or you may purchase a red clown nose to wear all day in honor of all red-nosed furry creatures!)

- Bring a box of reindeer food (carrots, grass, etc.) to leave out for Santa's reindeer.

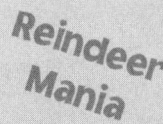

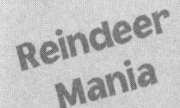

- Construct a semantic map or web with all the facts your students know about reindeer. Then ask them to list what they want to learn about reindeer as the day progresses.

Historical Background

The creator of "Rudolph, the Red-Nosed Reindeer" was Bob May. His four-year-old daughter, Barbara, wanted to know why her mother who was dying from cancer was different from other mothers. Bob May had experienced the feeling of being different, growing up smaller than other boys. One night, this gentle father told his daughter the story of a reindeer who felt different from those around him. The story was a hit with his daughter and became so popular he was encouraged to have it published. Handed down from generation to generation, it became one of our most beloved Christmas stories.

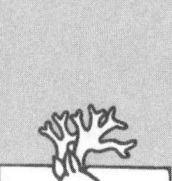

Literary Exploration

The Caribou by Jerolyn Nentl
How the Reindeer Saved Santa by Carolyn Haywood
Lapps: Reindeer Herders of Lapland by Alan James
Reindeer by Emery Bernhard
Reindeer Christmas by Moe Price
The Reindeer People by Ted Lewin
Rudolph Shines Again by Robert Lewis May, et al
Rudolph, the Red-Nosed Reindeer by Eileen Daly
Rudolph, the Red-Nosed Reindeer by Barbara Shook Hazen
Rudolph, the Red-Nosed Reindeer by Robert L. May, et al
Santa's Moose by Syd Hoff
Snipp, Snapp, Snurr and the Reindeer by Maj Lindman
The Snowy Path: A Christmas Journey by Lark Carrier
Where's Prancer? by Syd Hoff
The Wild Christmas Reindeer by Jan Brett

Language Experience

- Challenge students to write new words using the letters in *Rudolph, the Red-Nosed Reindeer.*

- Create a class Venn diagram with similarities and differences between a reindeer and a horse.

- Have students list Santa's reindeer (Dasher, Dancer, etc.), then alphabetize them.

Writing Experience

- Have students write about the year Rudolph couldn't fly! They can use the reproducible on page 38 or write their stories inside a flip-top head of Rudolph which they can make on brown construction paper with Rudolph's face and antlers made by tracing around their spread-out hands on tan construction paper.

- Let students write, "Advice from Rudolph" from Rudolph's point of view.

Science/Health Experience

- Study reindeer and their habitat. Reindeer are in the caribou family, are generally three to three and one-half feet tall, have wide antlers and can swim well. They live on moss that grows under the snow during the winter. Their milk can be made into cheese, and they are used to pull heavy sleds in some parts of the world.

Social Studies Experience

- Research areas of the world where reindeer may be found.

Music/Dramatic Experience

- Sing the old familiar favorite, "Rudolph, the Red-Nosed Reindeer!"

- Simple antlers can be made to fit on student heads so they can pantomime how Rudolph felt when others teased him. Let students pantomime the story as you sing it together.
Copy the antlers on page 39 on tan card stock. Cut them out and glue them to a paper headband.

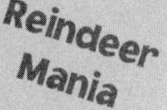

TLC10465 Copyright © Teaching & Learning Company, Carthage, IL 62321-001

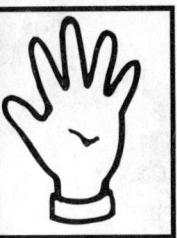

Physical/Sensory Experience

- Play Rudolph Tag. Start with two student "Rudolphs" running around. With Christmas getting closer, "Rudolph" needs more reindeer help, so he enlists the help of those he can "catch" to help pull Santa's sleigh. Each "Rudolph" tries to add as many reindeer on his or her team as possible. (Each "reindeer" holds onto the waist of the reindeer in front of him.) The team with the most reindeer wins!

- Blindfold one student at a time to play Pin the Red Nose on Rudolph (like Pin the Tail on the Donkey). See pattern on page 40.

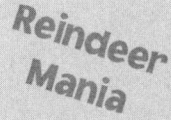

Arts/Crafts Experience

- A Candy Cane Rudolph can be made by gluing wiggly eyes, a red pom-pom nose and brown pipe cleaner antlers around the crook of the candy cane.

- Let students make a sleigh for Rudolph to pull by gluing two pipe cleaners (sleigh runners) to a painted egg carton section. After the paint is dry, the sleigh can be filled with goodies! You may prefer to use two small candy canes for the sleigh runners.

- Students can make Rudolph puppets by gluing two twig antlers to a decorated brown triangle head glued to a craft stick holder.

- Have students make reindeer gift bags. They cut the top portion of one side of a brown lunch sack and make a triangular cut on the other side to form a reindeer nose when folded down. Add large wiggly eyes, a red pom-pom nose, brown antlers and a bow under the reindeer's chin. Fill the bags with small gifts, popcorn or candy!

- Students can make a reindeer ornament by painting three craft sticks brown, then gluing them together in a triangular shape. Add wiggly eyes, a pom-pom nose and pipe cleaner antlers! These can be hung on the Christmas tree.

Extension Activities

⚠ Here are some fun Rudolph snacks students will enjoy making and eating.

Rudolph Cheesecake

Cut cheesecake into pie piece sections. Add chocolate topping. Top with a cherry nose, pretzel antlers and sliced almond ears.

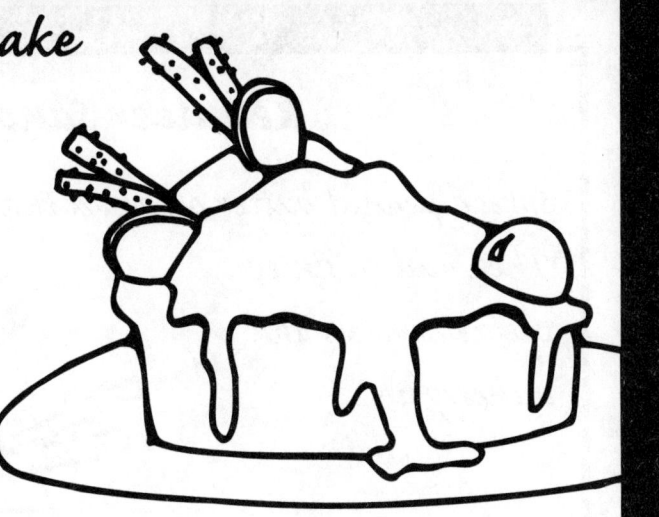

Reindeer Food

Mix one box of each of the following: thin pretzels, Cheerios™ and Wheat or Rice Chex™ cereal. Add 1 cup raisins and 1 cup of salted peanuts. Mix the above with the following: 1 stick margarine (melted), 2 T. soy sauce and Worchestershire sauce. Toss again and bake for about an hour at 325° F (stirring every 15 minutes).

Extension Activities continued

Reindeer Sandwiches

Spread peanut butter on bread that has been cut in triangles. Then add raisin eyes, pretzel antlers and a cherry nose.

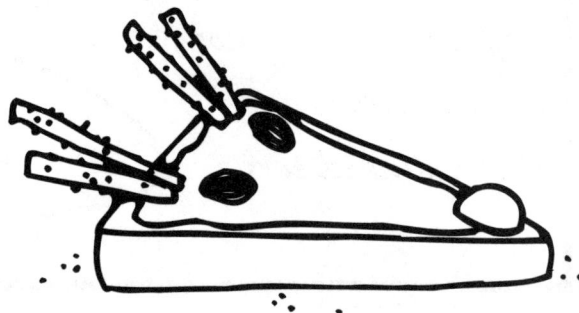

Reindeer Heads

Provide each student with a canned pear half (head base), raisins for eyes, a maraschino cherry nose and pretzel sticks for antlers. Let each student assemble their own reindeer head, then enjoy a fun treat!

Values Education Experience

- Encourage discussion about the effects of name-calling as the other reindeer did to Rudolph. Talk about how to be accepting of differences in people.

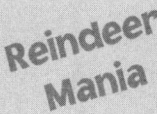

Reindeer Mania

Follow-Up/Homework Idea

- Encourage students to rent or check out the movie *Rudolph, the Red-Nosed Reindeer* to watch with their families.

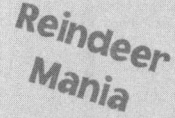

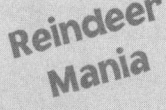

Reindeer Mania

The year Rudolph couldn't fly...

Name:

Martin Van Buren's Birthday

December 5

8TH PRESIDENT

Setting the Stage
- Display books about Van Buren, his vice presidency under Andrew Jackson and his own presidency.

Historical Background
Martin Van Buren, the eighth President of the United States, was born on this day in 1782. He was the first President born a citizen of the U.S.

Literary Exploration
Martin Van Buren: Eighth President of the United States by Rafaela Ellis
Martin Van Buren: Eighth President of the United States by Jim Hargrove

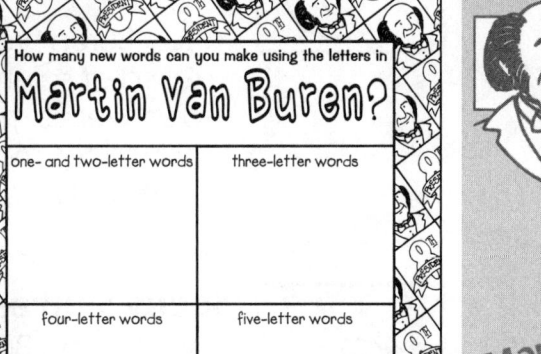

Language Experience
- How many new words can your students make using the letters in *Martin Van Buren*? See reproducible on page 44.

Writing Experience

- Since Martin Van Buren is a less familiar President, read one of the books listed on page 41 to your students. Then let them brainstorm words or give words used in the book to describe America's eighth President. List the words on the board. Once they have a working knowledge of him, challenge students to write cinquain poems about him, following these instructions:

Cinquain

An unrhymed poem of five lines:
Line 1: one word that names the subject
Line 2: two words that describe the subject
Line 3: three "ing" verbs that describe actions related to the subject
Line 4: four words that express a feeling about the subject
Line 5: one word that describes or renames the subject

Write the instructions on the board for students to see as they write. If you teach younger students, let them work together on a group cinquain poem.

Math Experience

- Martin Van Buren was born in 1782 and died in 1862. See how quickly students can figure out how old he was when he died. His four-year presidency began in 1837. Have them quickly figure out when his term of office ended. Create other correlated math problems for students to solve.

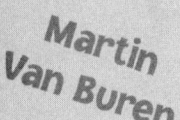

Science/Health Experience

- Martin Van Buren was only about 5' 6" tall. Have students research to find out the height of the other Presidents. Where would he fit in the lineup of short to tall Presidents?

- Van Buren was President from 1837 to 1441. What happened in the world of science during his presidential term? Were any interesting discoveries made? Any valuable inventions patented? Any medical advances made? Have students research those four years to see what they can find.

Social Studies Experience

- Martin Van Buren was born in New York state and after his presidency he went back home where he lived until his death. Have students find New York on a United States map. Explain that his home at Kinderhook, New York, overlooked the Hudson River. See if students can find Kinderhook on a New York map.

- Challenge students to find out if any other Presidents came from New York. (Millard Fillmore, Theodore Roosevelt, Franklin Roosevelt)

Music/Dramatic Experience
- Choose a student to be the president. Let other students be reporters asking the president questions at a news conference. They can ask anything they want, and the student answers the way he or she would if president for a day. After a few minutes, choose another student to act as president and let the previous president become a reporter. To make things interesting, play a cassette or CD of "Hail to the Chief" as each new president stands up.

Arts/Crafts Experience
- Your students will enjoy working together to make a time line of U.S. Presidents around the room. Use long sheets of white shelf paper. Assign each student a President to research, then draw on the time line and add relevant information. Those who get done with their work before others are done can work on a second President. To save time, you can duplicate pictures of the Presidents and have students glue them on the time line. When the time line is completed, students will be able to get a better idea of where Martin Van Buren fits into the long line of American Presidents.

Extension Activities
⚠ Bring cupcakes and punch to class and have a birthday party for Martin Van Buren. Have students sing "Happy Birthday" to him, then enjoy the treat.

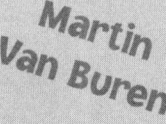

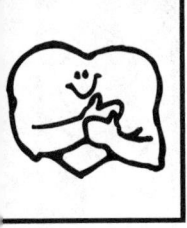
Values Education Experience
- Martin Van Buren was described as a gentle, kind man. Discuss the character a person needs to be President of the United States. Are gentleness and kindness important characteristics of our national leader? Why or why not? What do students think are the most important character traits a President should have?

Follow-Up/Homework Idea
- Encourage students on their way home today to try to remember the names of all the United States Presidents.

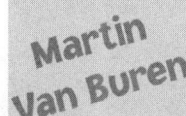

How many new words can you make using the letters in Martin Van Buren?

one- and two-letter words	three-letter words

four-letter words	five-letter words

six-letter words	seven-letter words

No More Slavery Day

December 6

Setting the Stage

- On a bulletin board put cut-out letters saying: "Free at Last! No More Slavery." Add the date: December 6, 1865. Beneath the board place a table with books and copies of articles about slavery in America and the Thirteenth Amendment. Have students draw pictures and make signs to express their feelings about slavery and mount them on the board.

- Construct a semantic web with facts your students know (or would like to know) about slavery.

Historical Background

On this day in in 1865, the Thirteenth Amendment to the United States Constitution was ratified, abolishing slavery. President Abraham Lincoln had announced the Emancipation Proclamation, declaring slaves in Confederate territory free on January 1, 1863, but the law was not passed until almost two years later.

Literary Exploration

Escape from Slavery: The Boyhood of Frederick Douglass in His Own Words by Frederick Douglass
Escape into the Night by Lois Walford Johnson
Go Free or Die: A Story About Harriet Tubman by Jeri Ferris
Harriet Tubman: Conductor on the Underground Railroad by Ann Petry
Letters from a Slave Girl by Mary E. Lyons
Meet Addy: An American Girl by Connie Rose Porter
Nightjohn by Gary Paulsen
A Picture of Freedom: The Diary of Clotee, a Slave Girl by Patricia C. McKissack
Steal Away by Jennifer Armstrong
They Came in Chains: The Story of the Slave Ships by Milton Meltzer
Uncle Tom's Cabin by Harriet Beecher Stowe

Language Experience

- Read excerpts from Frederick Douglass' book *Escape from Slavery: The Boyhood of Frederick Douglass* to give your students a personal account of slavery from one who experienced it. Then challenge students to remember specific words (such as adjectives) Douglass used to describe his experience. List the words on the board and discuss them.

- Have students look up the term *underground railroad* in the dictionary. Discuss what it was. Then ask students why they think it was called such an unusual name. Analyze the words together.

Writing Experience

- Explain that Phyllis Wheatly was the first important African American poet. She was brought to Boston on a slave ship in about 1800 at the age of 8. She was bought by kind people who taught her to read and write. She began writing poetry at age 14. Later in life, she was freed and got married. After discussing slavery and reading at least one of the books listed on page 45 to the class, challenge students to imagine themselves in a slavery situation. What would they write about in a poem about their lives as slaves? Have each student write a short poem (at least four lines), rhymed or unrhymed about slavery or getting free from slavery.

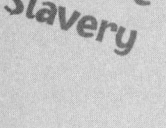

- Ask students to think about their freedom. How do they spend their time each day after school and on weekends? Does someone keep watch over them to make sure they are doing exactly what someone else tells them to do? Does anyone tell them what they can or cannot be when they grow up? Does anyone tell them how they can or cannot spend their money? Does anyone make them work, without pay, from morning until night? (Going to school doesn't count!) Let them try to express what *personal freedom* means to them.

- Have students write essays on the topic: "Every Person Should Be Free." Encourage them to express their ideas and personal convictions and tell why they feel this way. Their essays can go on the bulletin board described on page 45.

- Use the pattern on page 50 for students' writing.

Math Experience

- Pose the following math problems for your students to solve:

  Frederick Douglass was born in February 1817. He died in February 1895. How old was he when he died? (1895 – 1817 = 78 years old)

  On August 11, 1841, Frederick Douglass, a slave who had escaped to freedom only three years earlier, spoke at an antislavery convention in Massachusetts. His speech was so well done and so informative, he was asked to become a full-time speaker to represent the Massachusetts Anti-Slavery Society. He became famous for his lectures and writings about the rights of black people and of all human beings. What year did Mr. Douglass escape from slavery? (1841 – 3 years = 1838)

  On this day the Thirteenth Amendment to the United States Constitution was ratified, abolishing slavery. President Abraham Lincoln announced the Emancipation Proclamation on January 1, 1863, but the law was not passed until almost two years later. When was slavery officially abolished? (1863 + 2 = 1865)

  How many years ago was slavery abolished?
  (this year – 1865 = _____ years ago)

- Come up with other correlated math problems for students to solve.

Science/Health Experience

- Talk about how the south fueled its economy with slave labor in the cotton fields. Cotton became extremely profitable after Eli Whitney invented his cotton gin in 1793. Have students research the cotton gin to find out what it was and how it worked. Point out that most large farms in the south raised cotton, and since there was no machinery to pick the cotton, many hand-pickers were needed. Would cotton growers have gone broke paying cotton pickers?

- Bring some cotton to class for students to see, or show pictures of people picking cotton. Find out where cotton is grown today and how it is picked.

Social Studies Experience

- This is a good time to introduce or review the Civil War, emphasizing the reason for it.

- Tell students that by 1860, when the Civil War began, most United States slaves lived in the south, serving on cotton plantations. The states with the largest slave populations were Virginia, Mississippi, Alabama and Georgia. Have students find these four states on a United States map.

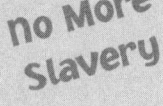

- Slavery began in America in the 1600s. Many Americans turned against it during the American Revolution, feeling everyone deserved freedom. Some national leaders such as George Washington and Thomas Jefferson spoke out against slavery even though they owned slaves. Have students research these two men to find out more about their beliefs about slavery.

- Let interested students research Harriet Tubman and the Underground Railroad. Have them report their findings to the rest of the class.

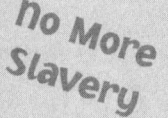

Music/Dramatic Experience

- Play some examples of black spirituals for your students. Explain that many of these songs were sung by slaves as they worked in the fields. (Examples: "Swing Low, Sweet Chariot," "Deep River" and "Nobody Knows the Trouble I've Seen.") You may also want to play some of the songs sung about escaping to freedom, such as "Follow the Drinking Gourd" which referred to escaping slaves following the big dipper in the sky for direction as they ran away.

- Find a recording of the 1960s folk song "In Them Old Cotton Fields Back Home" and play it for your class.

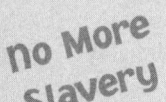

Physical/Sensory Experience

- Sing the old folk song: "Jump down, turn around, pick a bail of cotton" or play a tape or CD of it for students to learn. Have them sing it together and go through the motions described in the song, pretending to pick cotton.

Arts/Crafts Experience

- Let students illustrate the work of the underground railroad in a classroom mural. Stretch white shelf paper across one wall. Let students decide what kinds of scenes they want to include in the mural. Assign each student a section of the mural to draw. When it's done, invite parents and other classes to come and see it.

- Challenge each student to design a memorial to the end of slavery. It can be a building, a statue or other design that will go in a prominent place in our nation's capital. Have students plan their ideas and sketch them on paper. When they are done, have students show their ideas to the class and explain them. Mount the ideas on a wall and number each one. Hand out slips of paper and have students vote on the memorial they think should be in Washington, D.C.

- Explain to your class that bells such as the Liberty Bell are one symbol of freedom. Let students make individual freedom bells to hang all over the room to celebrate freedom. Copy bell patterns on cardstock. Have students color and cut out two apiece. They cut a slit up the middle of one bell from the bottom halfway up and from the top halfway down on the other one. Then they match the slits and put the bells together to form one bell. See the patterns on page 51.

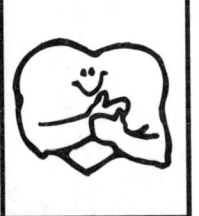

Values Education Experience

- Ask students how we should treat one another. Should anyone have the right to completely control another person? Discuss the goals of helping others and showing kindness instead of only caring about what we can get from people.

Follow-Up/Homework Idea

- Have students go home and express to their families how grateful we should all be for our personal freedom as well as our national freedom.

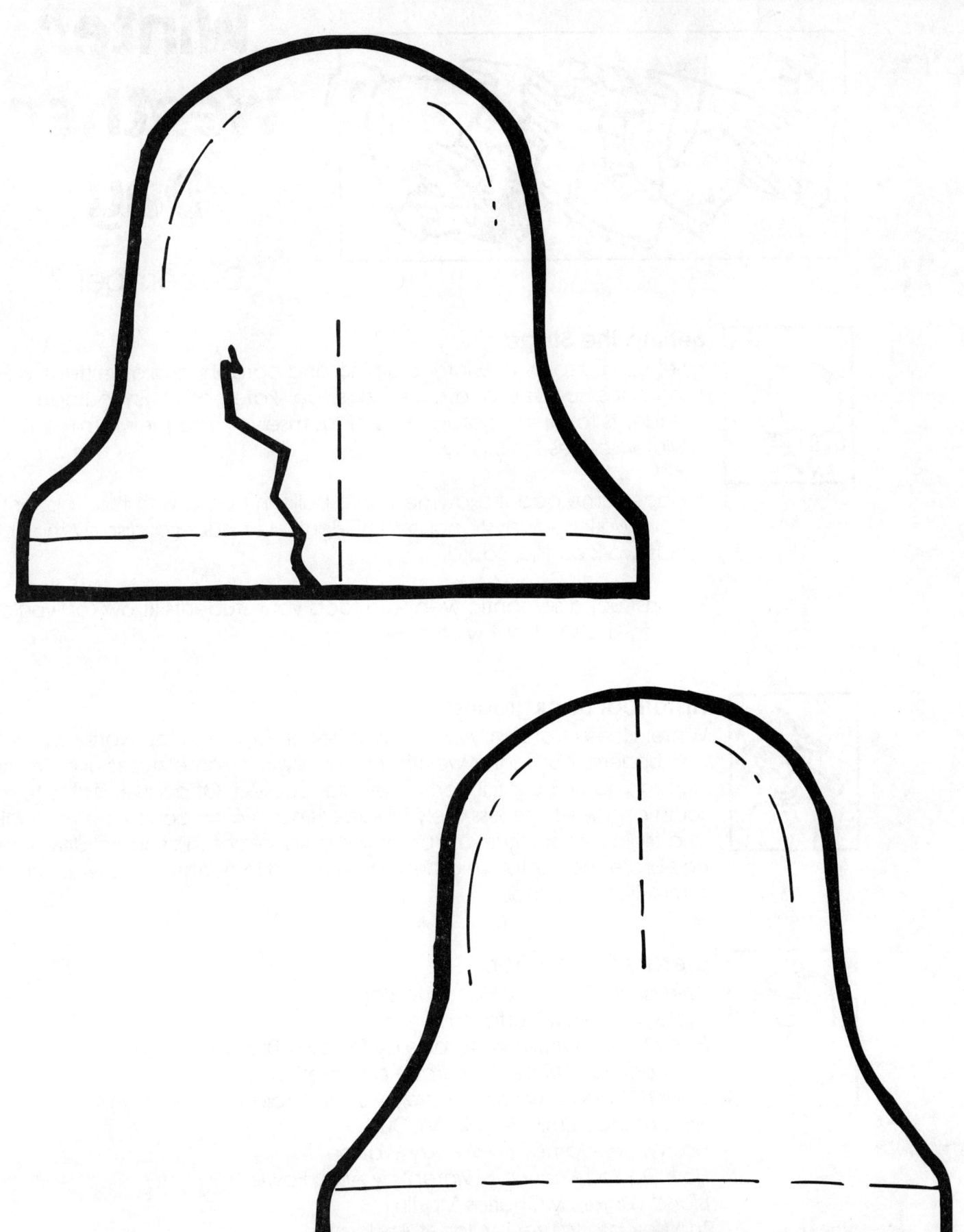

Winter Weather Day

December 7

Setting the Stage

- Set up a display of winter clothing and paraphernalia (mittens, stocking caps, scarves, boots, sled, skiis, ice skates, etc.). Encourage students to bring photographs of themselves and their families in winter scenes to display.

- Place some paper snowmen on a bulletin board with the caption: "Our Work Is Always Cool and BRRight!" Let students display their best classwork on the board.

- Construct a semantic web with facts your students know (or would like to know) about winter.

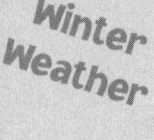

Historical Background

Winter doesn't officially begin until December 21 in the Northern Hemisphere, but winter weather may begin in some states in November, depending on how far north they are located. Of course, states farther south and west are less likely to experience wintry conditions (snow, ice and frigid temperatures). But for the purposes of this special day, we will celebrate the winter weather experienced in northern, midwestern and some western states.

Literary Exploration

Animals in Winter by Henrietta Bancroft
The Big Snow by Berta Hader
Buzzy Bear's Winter Wardrobe by Dorothy Bronson Marino
Clementine's Winter Wardrobe by Kate Spohn
Dear Rebecca, Winter Is Here by Jean Craighead George
First Snow by Emily Arnold McCully
Has Winter Come? by Wendy Watson
How Do You Know It's Winter? by Allan Fowler
Island Winter by Charles Martin
The Key into Winter by Janet Anderson
The Last Snow of Winter by Tony Johnston
Lucy's Winter Tale by Amy Ehrlich
Max and Maggie in Winter by Janet Craig

Literary Exploration continued

Snow Is Falling by Franklyn M. Branley
Snowplows by Hope Irvin Marston
Snow Day: Stories and Poems by Caroline Feller Bauer
The Snowy Day by Ezra Jack Keats
Warm in Winter by Erica Silverman
We Celebrate Winter by Bobbie Kalman
When Winter Comes by Robert Maass
White Wonderful Winter! by Elaine Good
Why Won't Winter Go? by Lissa McLaughlin
Wild Horse Winter by Tetsuya Honda
Winter Barn by Peter Parnall
The Winter Day by Beverly Komoda
Winter Harvest by Jane Chelsea Aragon
The Winter Noisy Book by Margaret Wise Brown
Winter Picnic by Robert Welber
A Winter Place by Ruth Radin
A Winter's Journey by David Updike
Winter: Tracks in the Snow by Janet McDonnell

Language Experience

- Brainstorm adjectives to describe winter. List them on the board as students say them. Then have students put the words in alphabetical order.

- Create a class Venn diagram with similarities and differences between winter in the state where you live and a state in a different part of the country.

Writing Experience

- Students will enjoy writing about winter from the viewpoint of a snowman in the yard. They should get a whole different perspective on cold weather!

- Let students write short stories, choosing from these story starters:

    I rolled the big snowball and it kept getting bigger and bigger. Then suddenly, it began rolling down the hill and taking me with it!

    Gliding across the snow on my skiis, I tried to stop when a bear suddenly stepped out in front of me. But it was too late!

    Sadly I sat in my room looking out my window at the new-fallen snow. Mom wouldn't let me go out with my bad cold. Then I saw something I could hardly believe!

    It was snowing when I went to bed, and when I woke up everything was silent. I looked out my window, but couldn't see anything because our house was completely covered with snow!

Math Experience

- Have students figure out in how many days it will officially be winter. Have them draw their answer in snowmen.

- Have students count the number of students in your classroom, then figure out how many mittens would be needed to cover every hand. Have them draw the correct number of mittens to show the answer.

Science/Health Experience

- Study animal adaptation to climate changes. Discuss hibernation and migration.

- Do some experiments with water as it freezes to discover characteristic properties of water.

- Study weather. What conditions are necessary for snow?

- Have students research to discover the average winter temperature in your area and the average winter snowfall. Compare these numbers with that of other places in the country and in the world.

- Discuss what birds do for food and shelter in the winter. Decorate a tree in your school yard with food for the birds. String popcorn or cereal and hang it on the tree. Spread peanut butter on pinecones, then roll them in birdseed. Attach string or fishing line to them and hang them in the tree. Buy a suet cake and hang it. Then put your students on the alert to watch in coming days to see if they recognize the birds who come to eat the snacks.

Social Studies Experience

- Remind students that while North America is having winter, other parts of the world are having summer. Show a world map or hold up a globe and have students point out which areas are having winter and which are having summer.

TLC10465 Copyright © Teaching & Learning Company, Carthage, IL 62321-0010

Music/Dramatic Experience

- Play a cassette or CD of the familiar holiday song "Winter Wonderland." Discuss the different aspects of winter mentioned in the song. (sleigh, snow, bluebird gone, snowman, fire, etc.)

- Challenge students to work in pairs to compose songs to familiar tunes to celebrate winter weather. Use a tune such as "Row, Row, Row Your Boat." When the songs are completed, sing them together.

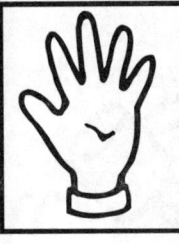

Physical/Sensory Experience

- Take a nature walk and have students look for signs of winter. Have them take along paper and pencils so they can make observational drawings along the way.

- If you live in an area where it snows, talk about what it's like when it snows: the sounds boots make when you walk on the snow, the sound of the wind, the silence that comes during a calm snow, the feel of snow or sleet hitting your face, the feeling of snowflakes on your tongue, the cold feeling in your hands when you're making snowballs, the warm feeling when you go back inside and wrap up in a blanket or drink hot chocolate, etc. If it's snowing today, take your class outside for a few minutes to experience all these senses.

Arts/Crafts Experience

- Let your students try their hands at bare birch paintings. They blow through a drinking straw to spread white tempera paint across the bottom of a sheet of dark blue construction paper. The paint will thin out as it is blown upwards, creating the branches of the birch tree. After the paint dries, students can use markers to add black marks on the birch tree branches. Have them mount their designs on black construction paper for a beautiful wintry effect.

- ⚠ Here's an idea for a different art medium! Have students make edible snowflakes by folding a flour tortilla three times, then tearing a snowflake design in it. When they unfold the tortilla, they'll have an interesting snowflake. They can sprinkle a little powdered sugar on the top, then eat their artwork!

TLC10465 Copyright © Teaching & Learning Company, Carthage, IL 62321-0010

Extension Activities

⚠ Let students make snowman snacks. Give each one three large marshmallows, some toothpicks, raisins or chocolate chips, a graham cracker, vanilla icing and two peppermint sticks. They stick the marshmallows together with the toothpicks; then add features with the raisins or chocolate chips. They stick the snowman on the graham cracker stand with icing, then add the peppermint sticks for the runners of the "sled." They can enjoy it, then eat it later!

⚠ Students can make edible snowflakes. Give each student a large marshmallow, 18 miniature marshmallows and 18 toothpicks. They stick the toothpicks all over the large marshmallow, then stick mini marshmallows on the other ends. If they're careful, they can even add more toothpicks to the mini marshmallows and stick on additional mini marshmallows for another layer!

⚠ A cup of hot chocolate in the wintertime is a wonderful treat. Give each student two large marshmallows and a toothpick. They can make a snowman to float in the cup of hot chocolate you give each of them. If they want to add a face to the snowman, provide food coloring. They can dip toothpicks into the food coloring and draw a face on the marshmallow snowman.

Values Education Experience

- Point out to students that winter is a great time to make new friends. Discuss some ways to make friends, reaching out to other people. Talk about inviting friends to play, to help build a snowman or make snow angels, to share some hot chocolate, to go to a movie or ball game, etc. Then discuss characteristics of a friend: loyal, friendly, willing to listen, shares, accepts, etc.

Follow-Up/Homework Idea

- Encourage students to look around them on their way home today. What signs of winter do they see? How are people coping with the changes winter brings? If you live in an area where the weather does not change a lot during winter, have students imagine how their trip home would be different if there was snow on the ground or if it was 20°F outside. Have students suggest that their families share some hot chocolate tonight.

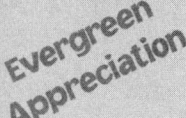

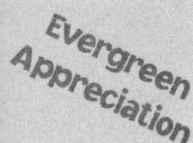

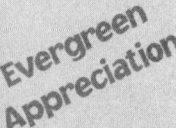

Evergreen Appreciation Day

December 8

Setting the Stage

- Gather pictures of all kinds of evergreens and display them on a wall above a table of books on the topic. Create a border around the display by tacking up an evergreen garland.

- Bring a small, live evergreen tree or an artificial one to display. Decorate it with natural items such as pinecones, berries, old birds' nests, grape vines, bird feathers, etc.

- Display your students' classwork on a bulletin board covered with green. Mount each paper on a tree shape. Add the caption: "We Do Tree-Mendous Work!"

- Construct a semantic map or web with facts your students know (or would like to know) about evergreens.

Literary Exploration

The After-Christmas Tree by Linda Tyler
The Beautiful Christmas Tree by Charlotte Zolotow
The Biggest Christmas Tree on Earth by Fernando Krahn
Christmas Tree Farm by David Budbill
Christmas Tree on the Mountain by Carol Fenner
Christmas Trees by Kathy Henderson
The Little Fir Tree by Margaret Wise Brown
The Miracle Tree by Christobel Maltingley
Surprise in the Mountains by Natalie Carlson
The Tree by Judy Hindley

Language Experience

- How many words can your students think of that rhyme with *tree*? Write the words on the board, then have them alphabetize the list.

- Write the word *evergreen* on the board. Explain that it is a compound word. Break it into its two parts, then put it back together. Have students brainstorm other compound words. List them on the board and discuss each one.

Writing Experience

- Let students imagine that they are evergreen trees in the woods. How do they feel when someone comes and chops them down, puts them in a truck and takes them to a city lot where Christmas trees are sold? Challenge students to express their ideas and feelings from the trees' perspective.

- Invite students to each write a description of an evergreen tree for someone who has never seen one before. They should describe the leaves or needles, the pinecones, the shape of the tree, the smell, etc.

Math Experience

- Take your class to a lot where Christmas trees are sold. Take along tape measures and let students have fun with measuring activities. They can measure the heights of the trees and compare them. Challenge them to find the tallest tree and the shortest one. They can measure around the tree trunks and the width of the trees. Make sure you get permission from the lot manager for this activity.

Math Experience continued

- Use pine needles for math manipulatives. Give each student a bag of pine needles to count and sort by tens. When each student has a total, write all the totals on the board and have students determine the grand total of pine needles.

- Take students for a nature walk in an area where they can see some evergreen trees. Challenge them to count the pinecones on a tree.

Science/Health Experience

- Pot a small evergreen cutting and keep it in the classroom. Have students water it and take care of it to see if they can help it grow.

- Have students research in what kinds of climates most evergreens grow, then share their findings.

- Use a Venn diagram to show the similarities and differences between evergreen trees and deciduous trees. (Explain that a deciduous tree is one that drops its leaves, such as maples or oaks.)

Social Studies Experience

- Learn about places that grow Christmas trees to sell. Mark the places on a map.

- Hang bird and squirrel food on an evergreen in your school yard as a winter treat. Take students out to look at the tree later in the day to see how many feathered and furred visitors have come.

Music/Dramatic Experience

- Challenge students to work together to compose a class song in praise of evergreens to a familiar tune such as "London Bridge Is Falling Down." Write the lyrics of the song on the board and sing it together.

- Have students pretend they are evergreen trees growing in the forest. Have them talk to each other, expressing their feelings about being trees. Do they ever have visits from forest animals or birds? Are they happy staying where they are or would they like to be able to see lands beyond the forest? How do they spend their time each day? What is their favorite part of the day? Their favorite time of year? Encourage students to be creative and include humor in their conversations.

Physical/Sensory Experience

- Take students to a Christmas tree lot or to a park where there are various kinds of evergreens. Let them gently feel the trees to see how different kinds of trees have different textures. (Examples: the soft texture of white pine, the prickly texture of cedar, the sticky feel of some pines) Encourage students to smell the trees. Can they tell a difference in the scents of the various kinds?

Arts/Crafts Experience

- Make a "handy" evergreen tree. Hand out green construction paper of various shades. Have students trace their hands, with fingers spread out, and cut them out. Group the hands together in a tree shape on the wall. Add a trunk cut from brown paper.

Arts/Crafts Experience

- Students can make pinecone holiday trees. Let them glue beads, sequins, red hots and silver candy cake decorations to the layers on the pinecone. They can glue a gold star at the top, then place the pinecone tree on a paper saucer turned upside down. Let them add pieces of cotton batting around the base to resemble snow.

⚠ For an edible evergreen, students can spread green icing (vanilla icing with green food coloring in it) on a sugar cone, then place it upside down on a paper saucer. Let them add a garland of licorice whip and candy decorations such as: red hots, candy sprinkles, etc., if they like. They can "glue" the decorations on with more frosting. For a more natural looking tree, they can "glue" on mini chocolate chips to represent pinecones.

Arts/Crafts Experience continued

- Let students make stand-up evergreens by cutting two evergreen shapes exactly alike from green cardstock. Then they cut a slit from the bottom of one halfway up the middle, and from the top of the other halfway down the middle. They slip the two trees together to make an evergreen. Let students make several trees if time permits to take home and use as holiday decorations.

Extension Activities

- Take students to visit a tree farm. Ask the manager to provide information such as how long it takes for an evergreen to grow big enough to be sold for a Christmas tree, how the trees must be cared for, etc. Buy some evergreen branches to decorate your classroom.

- Holly is the only broad-leaved tree that is an evergreen. Bring some holly to class for students to enjoy and use to decorate the room.

Values Education Experience

- Remind students that evergreens are a part of our natural world that we need to care for and protect. They need clean air and good soil to grow. How can we keep this Earth a healthy place for people and plants and animals to grow? People are encouraged to recycle their Christmas trees every year instead of just throwing them in the trash. Talk about why recycling is a responsible way to live.

Follow-Up/Homework Idea

- Encourage students to get their families to go for a neighborhood walk tonight, looking for evergreens.

Joel Chandler Harris' Birthday

December 9

Setting the Stage

- Gather books by Joel Chandler Harris and display them along with stuffed animals (fox, rabbit, bear and wolf) to represent the animals he wrote about.

- Construct a semantic map or web with facts your students know (or would like to know) about Joel Chandler Harris.

Historical Background

On this day in 1848, American author Joel Chandler Harris was born in Georgia. He became known for his Uncle Remus stories which were first published in *The Atlanta Constitution*.

Literary Exploration

All Stuck Up by Linda Hayward
Nights with Uncle Remus by Joel Chandler Harris
Uncle Remus and His Friends by Joel Chandler Harris
Uncle Remus: His Songs and His Sayings by Joel Chandler Harris

Language Experience

- Read aloud some sections from an Uncle Remus story. Ask students if they understand the words. Explain that Joel Chandler Harris wrote his stories as if they were told by Uncle Remus, a former slave who was a servant of a southern family who entertained the children with animal fables. The way Harris wrote the stories is the way Uncle Remus, or any African American in the south in the 1800s, would have told them. This way of talking is called a *dialect*. People who live in different areas at different times speak in dialects. Ask students if they have friends or relatives who live in different parts of the country who say their words differently and use different expressions.

- Explain that the word *Brer* in Uncle Remus' stories is his way of saying, "*Brother.*"

Language Experience continued

- Let students see how many words they can make out of the letters in Joel Chandler Harris' name.

- Read one or two of Aesop's fables to the class. Compare the stories to the Uncle Remus stories. Which is easier to understand? Which do students like better? Why?

Writing Experience

- Explain that each animal story Uncle Remus told always taught a lesson, like Aesop's Fables. Read one of Uncle Remus' stories aloud. Then let students write their own animal stories to teach lessons. Remind them to make sure the lesson of the story is obvious. When the stories are done, have students read them aloud. Let the class guess what the lesson is in each story. See reproducible on page 68 for students' stories.

- Challenge students to write cinquains about Uncle Remus after they read about him. Print the following directions on the board for writing cinquains:

Cinquain

An unrhymed poem of five lines:
Line 1: one word that names the subject
Line 2: two words that describe the subject
Line 3: three "ing" verbs that describe actions related to the subject
Line 4: four words that express a feeling about the subject
Line 5: one word that describes or renames the subject

Let students read their poems aloud when they're done.

Science/Health Experience

- Study the lives of wild animals, especially bears, wolves, rabbits and foxes. Ask students why they think Joel Chandler Harris chose those animals for his stories. Brer Rabbit always seems to be the cleverest animal. Is that true in real life? Are rabbits clever? What animals do students think are the smartest? Why?

Social Studies Experience

- In the 1860s, Joel Chandler Harris worked as a printer on a plantation in Georgia. Many of the stories Uncle Remus tells are stories Harris heard from slaves on that plantation. Study southern plantations and slavery before the Civil War. Then study what happened to slaves after the war was over.

- Have students find the state of Georgia on a United States map. Study the history of the state, especially in the 1800s. Talk about slavery in the United States. Remind students that Georgia was a slave state and fought in the Confederacy against the North during the Civil War.

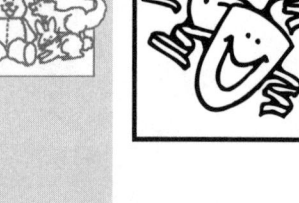

Music/Dramatic Experience

- Assign parts and let students act out some of Uncle Remus' stories as you read them aloud.

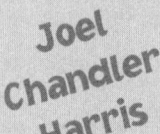

Arts/Crafts Experience

- Let students draw pictures of their favorite Uncle Remus characters.

- Hand out clay and let students sculpt Brer Rabbit's tar baby the way they think it looked!

Extension Activities

- Invite your school principal or other leader to visit your classroom and read some Uncle Remus stories to your students.

⚠ Let students help make "briar patch" cookies. Place one 8.5 oz can of chinese noodles in a large bowl. Melt one 12 oz package of chocolate chips in the microwave. Pour chocolate over noodles and mix until most of the noodles are covered. Drop by tablespoons onto a wax-paper-lined cookie sheet. Chill (or let stand) until chocolate hardens.

Values Education Experience

- Talk about the importance of being even-tempered. It was Brer Rabbit's angry temper that got him all stuck up to the tar baby. Ask students how losing our temper can cause problems. How can we be patient and even-tempered when people upset us?

Follow-Up/Homework Idea

- Tell students to try to tell their families one of Uncle Remus' stories in his dialect tonight.

Human Rights Day
December 10

Setting the Stage
- Allow students to help you with this bulletin board. Have them trace an outline of their hands on white construction paper and cut them out. Form the hand shapes into letters for the key words in the caption: "Our Hope for the World Is LOVE (or HAPPINESS).

- Construct a semantic web with facts your students know (or would like to know) about human rights.

Historical Background
In 1948 on December 10th the United Nations adopted the "Universal Declaration of Human Rights" which set forth basic rights and freedoms for all men and women in the world. The whole month of December has been set aside to spread the news of human rights throughout the world.

Literary Exploration
The Araboolies of Liberty Street by Sam Swope
Human Rights by Charles Freeman
Human Rights by Gerald Snyder
Human Rights by Jane Sherwin

Language Experience
- Ask students to brainstorm words they think of when they hear the term *human rights*. Write the words they suggest on the board. To get them started, ask: "What do all people everywhere deserve to have?" When the list is complete, discuss each word to make sure all the students understand it.

Writing Experience

- Discuss the U.N.'s definition of *human rights* (right to life, liberty and security; right to be educated; right to fair treatment with the law; freedom to worship; equal pay for equal work and freedom to have your own family). Let students pick one of these rights and explain what it means to them. They can write their ideas on the reproducible on page 74.

- Students can write for more information to:
  UN Public Info.
  United Nations, NY 10017

Social Studies Experience

- Research together the history and evolution of human rights.

- Discuss the rights and freedoms we have in the United States that people in many other countries don't have, such as the right to vote for our leaders. Ask students what countries they think don't have as many rights as they do.

- Look at a map of the world. Ask students to point out areas of the world where they think people may not have some of the basic human rights. Ask them to consider what it might be like living in those lands.

Music/Dramatic Experience

- Let students brainstorm other rights they think should be added to the list of human rights and make a short speech to defend their position.

- Sing the song, "Let There Be Peace on Earth" (words and music by Sy Miller and Jill Jackson).

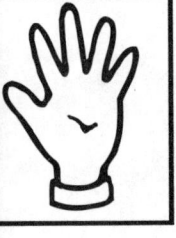

Physical/Sensory Experience

- Let students play a game of *Mother, May I*. After the game point out that in some countries people have to get permission to travel anywhere, to change jobs, to have children, etc. The leaders of these countries don't want their people to make any of their own decisions because they can control what happens when the people have no freedom of choice. These kinds of governments are called "totalitarian." The people are "totally" subject to the leaders.

71

Arts/Crafts Experience

- Let students design posters illustrating one or more of our basic human rights.

- Make a class display about human rights. List different people groups on the board:
    - Asian
    - African
    - South American
    - North American
    - Native American
    - Islander
    - European

Let students choose a kind of people to draw. Display the people drawings on a bulletin board with the caption: "All Humans Have Rights."

Extension Activities

- Depending upon the maturity level of your students, perhaps you could illustrate what it might be like without some of our human rights.

- If you know of a soldier on leave in your neighborhood, invite him or her to visit your class to talk about protecting freedom and human rights. Have the students express their thanks to the soldier for what he or she is doing.

Values Education Experience

- This is a great opportunity to remind students to be thankful for the freedoms they enjoy.

Indiana Statehood Day

December 11

Setting the Stage
- Display travel posters or brochures from a local travel agency depicting interesting information about the state of Indiana to get students excited about the day's emphasis.

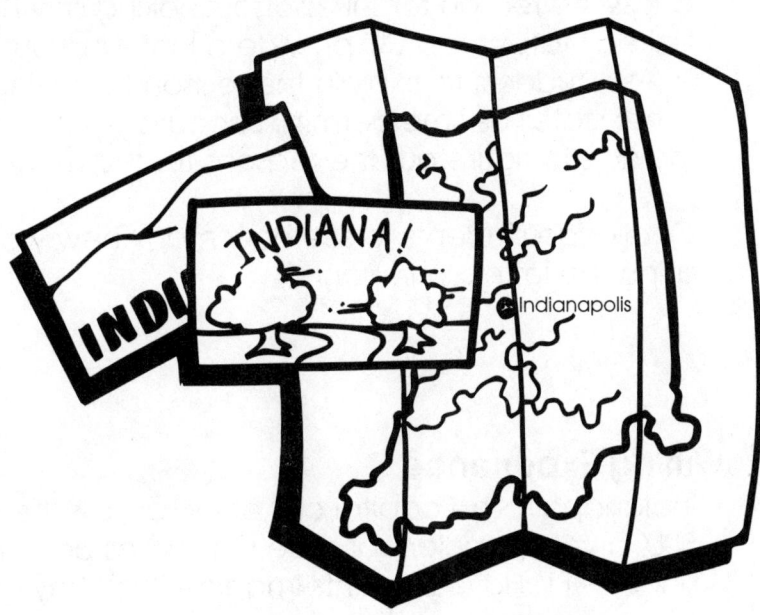

- Construct a semantic web with facts your students already know (or would like to know) about Indiana.

Historical Background
Indiana became the 19th state in the U.S.A on this day in 1816.

Literary Exploration

Indiana by Marlene Targ Brill
Indiana by Allan Carpenter
Indiana in Words and Pictures by Dennis B. Fradin
Log Cabin in the Woods: A True Story About a Pioneer Boy by Joanne Landers Henry, et al

Language Experience

- Most states have nicknames like people often do. Indiana's nickname is the Hoosier State. No one really knows where the name came from, but it's been around for many years. Have students find out the nicknames of other states, beginning with your own. If they can't find the origin of the nicknames, let them guess the reasons behind them. List the nicknames on the board next to the name of the states to which they belong.

- Indiana's state motto is "The Crossroads of America." Ask students to guess the reason for this motto. Looking at where Indiana is on a United States map will provide a hint. Find out what your state's motto is. Ask students to explain the reason for it. Find out the mottos of other states as time permits. Encourage students to use their reasoning skills to figure out the reasons for the mottos.

- Challenge students to see how many new words they can make using the letters in *Indiana*.

Writing Experience

- Indianapolis, the capital city of Indiana, is the site of the Indianapolis 500, a very popular car race which has been held every summer since 1911. Have students imagine that they get to see one of the races. Let them use their imagination to write about sitting in the huge crowd of spectators watching the race, hearing the roar of the engines and the yelling of the fans, with the sun beating down, etc. Students who have seen NASCAR events on TV will be able to imagine what it would be like to be there in person. Have any of your students attended a NASCAR race?

- Encourage students to write essays about living in Indiana. What would be good about it? What would not be so good? They can choose the exact city or rural area in which they would like to live.

Math Experience

- Hand out road maps of Indiana. Have students use rulers and the mileage chart on the maps to figure out how far it is from one place to another. (Examples: from Indianapolis to Evansville, from Michigan City to Ft. Wayne, etc.)

- The population of Indiana was 6,080,485 as of the 2000 census. Have students find out the population of your state and figure out the difference in the size of the population. (If you live in Indiana, choose a neighboring state for them to compare with.)

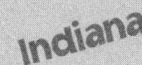

Science/Health Experience

- The average winter temperature in Indiana is from 27°F to 34°F. The average temperature in summer is between 75°F and 77°F. The average rainfall is from 36" to 43". The numbers vary because Indiana is a long state which has milder weather in the south than in the north. Have students find out the average winter and summer temperatures in your state and compare them with those of Indiana. Do the same with the average rainfall. (If you live in Indiana, choose another state to compare numbers with.)

Social Studies Experience

- Study the history of Indiana, beginning with the Native Americans there and the arrival of white explorers in 1679.

- Angel Mounds State Historic Site, near Evansville, pays tribute to the Missipian culture and the Native Americans who lived in this settlement between 1200 and 1450 A.D. Challenge students to learn more about this site and other mound-builder locations.

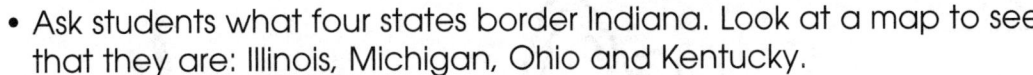

- Ask students what four states border Indiana. Look at a map to see that they are: Illinois, Michigan, Ohio and Kentucky.

- The state bird of Indiana is the cardinal. Have students research to discover how many other states have chosen the cardinal for their state bird.

Music/Dramatic Experience

- The first Raggedy Ann doll was created in Indianapolis in 1914. Bring a Raggedy Ann doll to class to show students or show them pictures from a catalog. Point out that the dolls are made with floppy arms and legs. Use Halloween makeup to paint students' faces like Raggedy Ann or Andy. Then play some music and let them pretend to be floppy dolls dancing to the music. They can walk, but with wobbly legs and their arms should flop around. Students will enjoy this activity, but you may need to keep a close watch so some of them don't get too rough.

Physical/Sensory Experience

- In 1871 the first professional baseball game was played in Ft. Wayne, Indiana. Divide students into two teams and let them pantomime a baseball game.

Arts/Crafts Experience

- One of the most famous towns in Indiana is Santa Claus. Every year the post office there receives about half a million packages and letters at Christmastime just to get the Santa Clause stamp on them. Have students draw comic strips of the Santa Claus post office two weeks before Christmas. Show them some comic strips from the newspaper so they'll see that the comic strip should show a developing situation. Words spoken by the comic strip characters should be in speech balloons. When the comic strips are completed, let students share them with one another. Have them draw their comic strips on the reproducible on page 79.

Extension Activities

- Indiana's chief agricultural product is corn. Have a corn-fest, letting students eat corn on the cob, creamed corn, cornbread, popcorn, corndogs and cornflakes.

Poinsettia Day

December 12

Setting the Stage
⚠ Please note: Many poison centers list the poinsettia plant as "mildly toxic." You should carefully monitor your students' contact with the plant and make sure that children do not bring their hands to their eyes or mouth if the plant has been touched. Make sure hands are washed thoroughly after the activity.

- Gather pictures of poinsettias and live poinsettia plants. Place them around a table on which you place related books and magazine articles.

- Construct a semantic map or web with facts your students know (or would like to know) about poinsettias.

Historical Background
Dr. Joel Roberts Poinsett, an American diplomat, introduced the poinsettia plant to the Unite States. The Central American plant was named after him and became a popular winter holiday plant in America.

Literary Exploration
Decking the Halls: The Folklore and Traditions of Christmas Plants by Linda Allen
The Gift of the Poinsettia by Pat Mora and Daniel Lechon
The Legend of the Poinsettia by Tomie de Paola
The Miracle of the First Poinsettia: A Mexican Christmas Story by Joanne Oppenheim
Poinsettias: Myth and Legend—History and Botanical Facts by Christian Anderson

Language Experience
- Print the word *poinsettia* on the board. Challenge students to make as many words as they can from the letters in the flower's name.

- Explain that the poinsettia was named after Dr. Joel Roberts Poinsett. Let students have some fun figuring out what flowers named after them would be called.

Writing Experience

- Let students write poems about the poinsettia plant. Write instructions for writing the poems on the board. Let students choose the kinds of poems they want to write.

Rhyme
At least four lines with the last word in every two lines or every other line rhyming

Acrostic
An unrhymed poem where the first letter in each line spells out the word *poinsettia*

Haiku
Three unrhymed lines with five syllables in the first and third lines and seven syllables in the second line

> (Example of Haiku:
> Poinsettias are great!
> Beautiful and colorful,
> Holiday flowers.)

- Have students write short stories about giving a poinsettia plant to a needy or lonely person during the holidays.

- The poinsettia has at least three other names: Christmas Flower, Lobster Flower, Mexican Flame Leaf. Have each student choose one of the names to write about. They can use their imagination to explain how the poinsettia got that name.

- See the pattern on page 85 on which students may write their poems or stories.

TLC10465 Copyright © Teaching & Learning Company, Carthage, IL 62321-0010

Math Experience

- Have students count the red, pink or white colored leaves on a poinsettia plant, then the green leaves. How many more colored leaves are there than green leaves? Have them count the tiny yellow flowers, too. They can record the numbers on a class graph and put today's date. Have them count again in a week, two weeks and three weeks and record the numbers to see if they change. The number of colored leaves should increase.

- Let students measure a poinsettia plant: its height, the length and width of its leaves, and the size of its flowers. If possible, have a dwarf poinsettia for them to measure as well as a normal sized one. (You may want to have them wear plastic gloves while measuring the plants since the leaves are poisonous and could cause a rash. Warn them not to touch their eyes before washing their hands.)

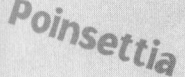

Science/Health Experience

- Explain that the leaves of the poinsettia plant are called "bracts." Write the word on the board. Many people think the leaves are the flowers of the poinsettia, but the flowers are actually the tiny, yellow dots in the very center of the plant. Let students carefully examine a poinsettia plant. Talk about what it needs to grow and stay healthy.

- Ask students if they have seen poinsettia plants in stores and offices (and even at home) recently. What colors are they? (red, pink and white)

- Tell students to be careful as they measure and examine poinsettias because the leaves are poisonous. They should always wash their hands immediately after touching the leaves. Explain that the leaves can also be toxic to pets, so they should place poinsettias at home off the floor so dogs can't touch them, and keep cats away from them.

- Poinsettias can grow up to 15 feet tall in their natural habitat in Mexico. The green leaves don't begin to change color until days grow shorter in the fall. Have students think of other plants that don't "bloom" until fall.

Arts/Crafts Experience

- Have students draw poinsettias on art paper with crayons, using lots of red and green. Then they can paint over the picture with black paint mixed with water. The poinsettias will resist the paint and the colors will pop out of the black background. Mount the pictures on the wall to decorate your classroom.

- Have students create poinsettia people with red, pink or white paper leaves for faces, stems for bodies and green leaves for arms and hands. Let them use their imagination to create whole poinsettia families.

- Hand out black, red, pink, white and green construction paper, scissors, glue and copies of the leaf patterns, page 84, on card stock for students to trace. Have each student cut out multiple copies of the leaves in their choice of colors. Then let them assemble the pieces into poinsettias on a black background. After they have their poinsettias arranged, they can glue the pieces down. Display the poinsettias around the room.

Extension Activities

- Take your class on a field trip to a florist to see a variety of poinsettia plants.

- ⚠ Give every student a slice of white bread, a plastic knife and some strawberry jam. Let them spread the jam on their bread to look like a poinsettia. Then they can eat their poinsettia treat.

Follow-Up/Homework Idea

- Encourage students to ask their parents if they can buy a poinsettia plant to give to a lonely neighbor or to a community helper such as the mail carrier to show their appreciation.

It's a Small World Day

December 13

Setting the Stage

- Display travel posters and brochures (from a local travel agency) around a large world map or globe for students to look at throughout the day.

- Let students look through a variety of magazines to find pictures of people from countries around the world. Display the pictures on a bulletin board with the caption: "It's a Small World." Have students bring photographs of themselves to add to the board.

- Construct a semantic map or web with facts your students know (or would like to know) about people in other countries.

Historical Background

On this day in 1577, Sir Francis Drake began his voyage around the world, a trip that took him three years. He and his 160 sailors in five ships were the first Englishmen to sail all the way around the globe. With new advances in communication technology and travel, the world seems to be shrinking more every year. What took Drake three years can now be done in hours by jet plane. Through e-mail we chat with people in China. On TV we see live broadcasts of events happening in the farthest corners of the world.

Literary Exploration

Around the World in a Hundred Years by Jean Fritz
The Book of Holidays Around the World by Alice Van Straalen
The Instant Answer Book of Countries by Annabel Warender
People by Peter Spier
Sir Francis Drake: His Daring Deeds by Roy Gerrard
Twenty-Two Splendid Tales to Tell from Around the World by Pleasant DeSpain
Wag-by-Wall by Beatrix Potter

Language Experience
- Teach students a greeting or to count to 10 in a foreign language.

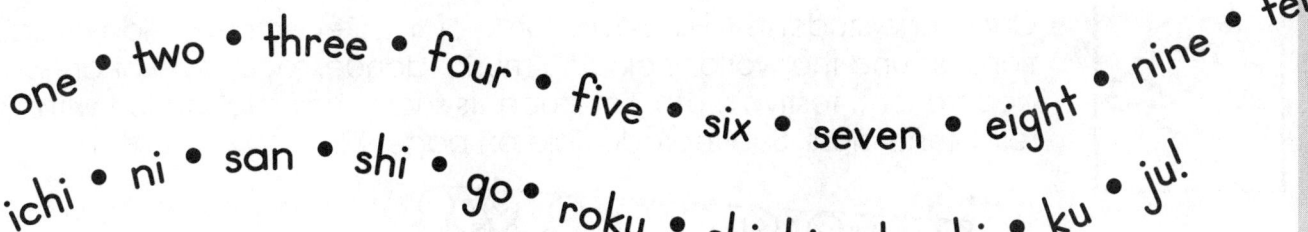

one • two • three • four • five • six • seven • eight • nine • ten!
ichi • ni • san • shi • go • roku • shichi • hachi • ku • ju!

It's a Small World

Writing Experience
- Have students write about where they would like to go to spend the holidays. See the reproducible on page 91.

- Let students imagine they have pen pals who live in another country. They can decide which country. Have each one write a letter to a pen pal, telling all about the country they live in and why it's a great place to live.

It's a Small World

Math Experience
- Bring some foreign currency to teach students about exchange rates between the United States and other countries. Let students see and handle the foreign money. Then hand out play money, such as from a Monopoly™ game. Write some imaginary exchange rates between another country and your country on the board. Then display some items or pictures of items they might want to buy. Label the items with prices from the other country. Have students figure out how much they would need to pay in their money for the items they would like to purchase.

It's a Small World

TLC10465 Copyright © Teaching & Learning Company, Carthage, IL 62321-0010

87

Science/Health Experience

- Ask students to choose a country they would like to visit. They need to know what to pack for the trip there, so challenge each student to find out what the weather is like in that country at this time of year. Is it warm or cold? Rainy or snowy? Then have them list the clothing and other items they would take with them on a trip to that country during the month of December. Discuss the differences or similarities between the weather where they live and the country they want to visit.

Social Studies Experience

- Challenge students to discover some of the December holiday traditions around the world, including music, dance, food, style of dress, decorations, festivals, etc. Let students share their information with the rest of the class. See reproducible on page 92.

- Talk about holiday traditions in this country that originated in other countries: holiday cookies and cakes from Europe, mistletoe from Scandinavia, poinsettias from Mexico, Christmas trees from Germany. Challenge students to discover others.

Music/Dramatic Experience
- Sing the Walt Disney song "It's a Small, Small World" (words and music by Richard and Robert Sherman).

Physical/Sensory Experience
- Let students try breaking a Mexican piñata filled with candy and other treats while you play a cassette or CD of Mexican music.

Arts/Crafts Experience
- Give each student two paper plates to color blue and green to resemble the Earth. Display a globe at the front of the room for them to look at as they draw the continent shapes on one side of the Earth (one paper plate), then switch the globe around as they draw the continents on the other side of the Earth (the second paper plate). Have them color on the bottom of the plates leaving the rims uncolored. They should print on the rim of the first plate: *It's a Small World*. On the rim of the second plate they should print: *Of People Who Are the Same*. Have them staple the plates together, then punch a hole in the top and loop string through it for a hanger. Discuss together how people all over the world may be different in the way they talk and dress and even look, but we're all the same in many ways. Discuss those ways.

Extension Activities

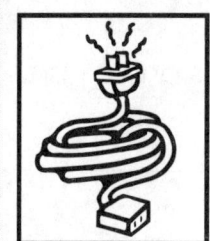

- Let students make passports just for play using their school pictures. Have them print the name of the country they are going to visit on the passports and fill out the personal information. Then they can fold their passports and keep them handy to have them stamped at the end of their trip. Arrange students' seats to resemble the interior of an airplane, rows of seats separated by an aisle. The teacher can be the airline stewardess, explaining about the overhead compartments, oxygen mask, exits, warning of possible turbulence, etc. Provide an in-flight snack and invite them to look out the windows to see the country they're flying over. They can imagine the mountains of Switzerland or the Sahara Desert or the fjords of Norway. At the end of the flight, stamp their passports.

Values Education Experience

- Discuss the importance of accepting and welcoming people of other races and cultures. Talk about the valuable contributions people from other countries have made to the American culture. (Food examples: pizza from Italy, egg rolls from China, tacos from Mexico)

Follow-Up/Homework Idea

- Encourage students to pretend on the way home tonight that they are taking a trip to another country.

Name: _____

Where in the world would you like to travel on the HOLIDAYS?

Holidays Around the World

Name: _____

Country I have chosen:

Research the country's holiday traditions and write them below:

Destinations		photo	PASSPORT
		Name	
		Address	UNITED STATES OF AMERICA
		signature	

Destinations		photo	PASSPORT
		Name	
		Address	UNITED STATES OF AMERICA
		signature	

South Pole Day

December 14

Setting the Stage

- Construct a semantic web with facts your students know (or would like to know) about the South Pole.

Historical Background

The Norwegian explorer, Roald Amundsen, led a dogsled expedition that reached the South Pole on this day in 1911.

Literary Exploration

Destination: Antarctica by Robert Swan
Fred's Pyramid by Stewart Moskowitz
Polar Animals by Norman Barrett
The Race to the South Pole by William Bixby
The Race to the South Pole by Rupert Matthews
Roald Amundsen and the Quest for the South Pole by Leo Flaherty
The True Story of Captain Scott at the South Pole by William Hollingsworth Wood

Language Experience
- How many words can your students think of that rhyme with the word, *pole*?

Writing Experience
- Let students write a packing list of items they would want to be sure and have with them on that their sled if they were part of Amundsen's team. See reproducible on page 97.

Science/Health Experience
- Temperatures have been known to reach -102°F at the South Pole. Discuss these extreme temperatures and the adaptations that would have to be made to survive in such a climate.

Social Studies Experience
- Let interested students research to find out more about Amundsen's expedition, then share their findings with the rest of the class. Trace his travels on a class map or globe.

Music/Dramatic Experience
- Sing some "cool" tunes today: "Frosty the Snowman" (words and music by Steve Nelson and Jack Rollins) and "A Marshmallow World" (words by Carl Sigman and music by Peter DeRose).

Arts/Crafts Experience
- Let students draw pictures of Roald Amundsen and his dogsled team
- Let students make masks of Amundsen and his dogs, attach each on a craft stick so they can hold them up to their faces and act out his story. See patterns on pages 98-99.

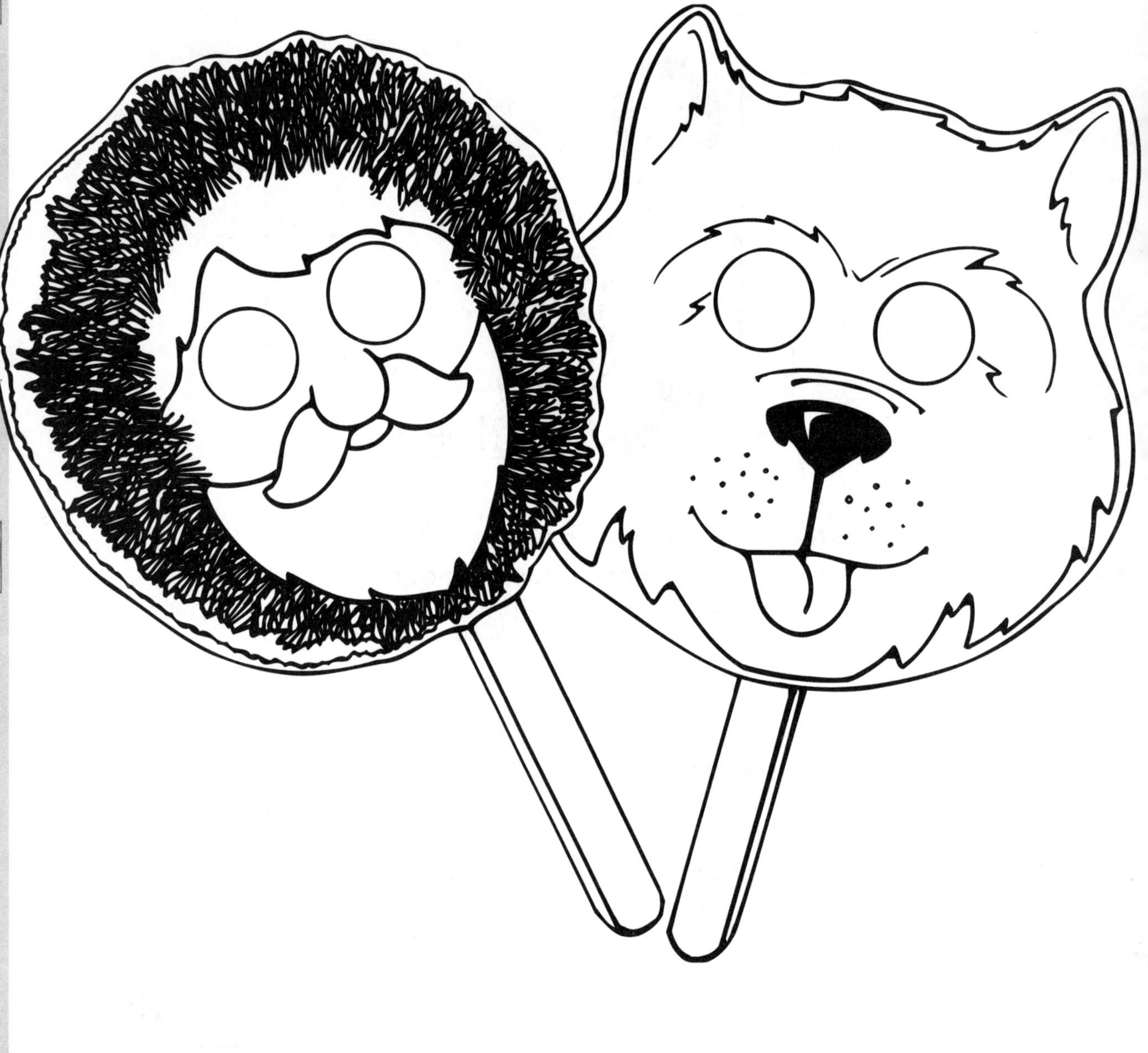

My packing list for my trip to the South Pole

Name:

Hanukkah Day

December 15
(varies)

Setting the Stage
- Greet students with "Shalom," the Hebrew greeting which means "peace."

- Borrow a menorah candle holder or dreidels to bring to class to display.

- Construct a semantic map or web with facts your students already know about Hanukkah, then invite them to ask questions about this religious holiday to help you structure the day's activities.

Historical Background
Hanukkah varies from year to year. It is celebrated for eight days beginning on the 25th day of the Hebrew month, Kislev. During a Jewish battle over religious freedom, the oil supply in the temple was dangerously low. The oil was needed to rededicate the temple and light the menorah lights. Miraculously, the small supply of oil lasted for eight days. Since then Jewish people throughout the world celebrate the miracle by lighting their own menorah, exchanging gifts, playing games and enjoying specially prepared foods. It is a time especially for Jewish families to spend time together and remember their blessings.

Literary Exploration

Arielle and the Hanukkah Surprise by Devra Speregen
Asher and the Capmakers: A Hanukkah Story by Eric A. Kimmel
Beni's First Chanukah by Jane Breskin Zalben
The Chanukkah Tree by Eric A. Kimmel
A Family Hanukkah by Bobbi Katz
The First Night of Hanukkah by Nicki Weiss
The Gift by Aliana Brodmann
A Great Miracle Happened There: A Chanukah Story by Karla Kuskin
Hanukkah by Dennis B. Fradin
Hanukkah by Miriam Nerlove
Hanukkah! by Roni Schotter
The Hanukkah Book by Marilyn Burns
My Hanukkah Book of Numbers by Claudia Kunin
Hanukkah Fun by Andrea R. Weiss
Hanukkah: The Festival of Lights by Jenny Koralek
Hanukkah Lights, Hanukkah Nights by Leslie Kimmelman
I Love Hanukkah by Marilyn Hirsh
In the Month of Kislev: A Story for Hanukkah by Nina Jaffe
Just Enough Is Plenty: A Hanukkah Tale by Barbara Diamond Goldin
Light Another Candle: The Story and Meaning of Hanukkah by Miriam Chaikin
The Miracle of Potato Latkes by Malka Penn
My Hanukkah Alphabet by Claudia Kunin
The Odd Potato: A Chanukah Story by Eileen Bluestone Sherman
One Yellow Daffodil: A Hanukkah Story by David A. Adler
The Picture Book of Hanukkah by David A. Adler
Poems for Jewish Holidays by Myra Cohn Livingston
Potato Pancakes All Around: A Hanukkah Tale by Marilyn Hirsh
The Uninvited Guest and Other Jewish Holiday Tales by Nina Jaffe
Your Neighbor Celebrates by Arthur Gilbert and Oscar Tarcov

Language Experience

- Hanukkah is called "The Festival of Lights." Brainstorm things related to lights.

Writing Experience
- As each candle is lit on the eight days of Hanukkah, family members exchange gifts. Ask students to write about what they would like to give or receive.

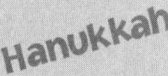 *Hanukkah*

Math Experience
- Have students measure candles of various lengths and put them in order from tallest to shortest. They can also measure the circumference of each one.

 *Hanukkah*

Social Studies Experience
- *Hanukkah* means "Festival of Lights." Explore the historical background of this holiday. Emphasize that people from around the world and other cultures celebrate many customs and holidays that are significant to their area and people. Discuss some others.

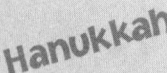 *Hanukkah*

Music/Dramatic Experience
- Sing songs from the book *Songs of Chanukah* by Jeanne Modesitt.

Physical/Sensory Experience

- Have students play with homemade dreidels they have made. (See below.) They sit in a circle and place shelled peanuts in the center as the "pot." As they spin the dreidel, it will land with a Hebrew letter showing. If the Hebrew letter, *nun* appears, the student receives nothing, If *hay* comes up, the player wins half the pot. If *gimmel* shows up the player gets all the peanuts. *Shin* means that a peanut must be put back in the pot.

- Play Pin the Candle on the Menorah (a variation of Pin the Tail on the Donkey).

Arts/Crafts Experience

- Students can make homemade Jewish dreidels by stapling shut small empty milk cartons from the lunchroom and covering them with paper. They draw a Hebrew letter on each side. A pencil speared through the top and bottom of the milk carton will serve as the spinning mechanism. To make this activity simpler, let them assemble the dreidel patterns on page 105. They fold the six squares and glue the tabs to form a cube, then stick a toothpick in the cube as shown.

- Let students make Hanukkah Star Hangings. Have them glue three craft sticks in a triangle then make a second triangle with three more craft sticks. They glue one triangle on the other to form a Star of David. After it dries, they loop a piece of yarn through it and hang it.

Extension Activities

⚠ Purchase Hanukkah gelt (gold, foil-covered candy coins) to give students.

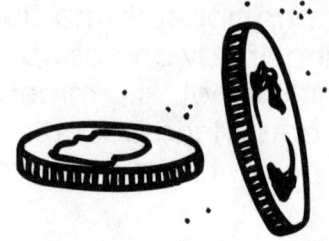

⚠ Have students make edible dreidels by inserting a toothpick into a large marshmallow with a chocolate kiss on the bottom.

• Invite a Jewish friend to visit your class and talk about Hanukkah.

⚠ Fry latkes, Jewish potato pancakes, in an electric frying pan with a little oil. Follow the recipe.

Latkes

In a large bowl, mix a dozen eggs, two large bags of frozen shredded hash brown potatoes, minced onion and salt and pepper to taste. Fry until golden brown. Serve with apple slices or applesauce.

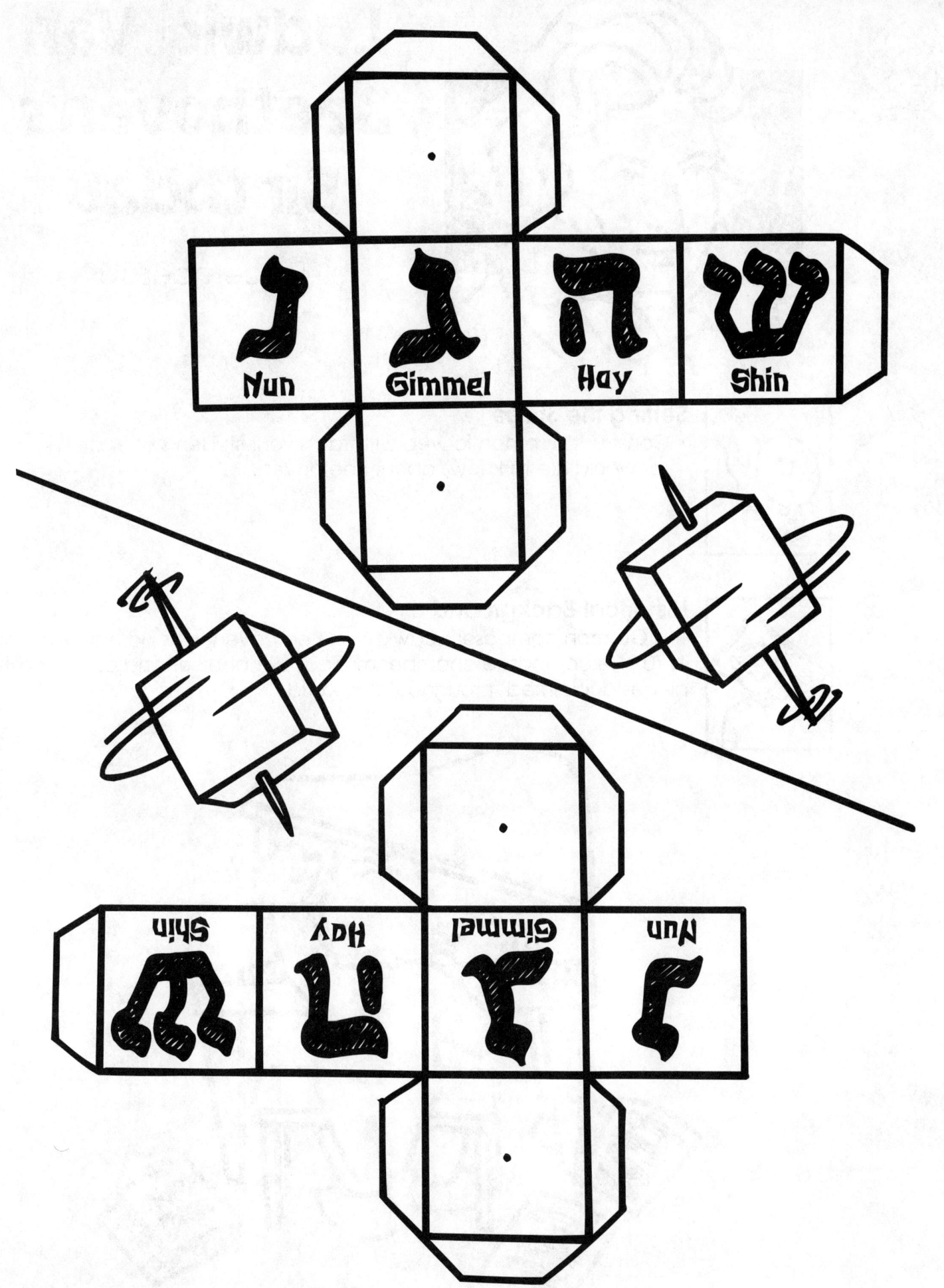

Ludwig Van Beethoven's Birthday

December 16

Setting the Stage
- Construct a semantic web with facts your students already know (or would like to know) about Beethoven.

Historical Background
The German composer, Ludwig Van Beethoven, was born on this day in 1770. He composed chamber musical, symphonies and piano masterpieces acclaimed throughout the world.

Literary Exploration
Beethoven by Alan Blackwood
Beethoven by David Jacobs
Beethoven by Nancy Loewen
Beethoven by Ann Rachlin
Beethoven Lives Upstairs by Barbara Nichol
Ludwig Van Beethoven by Noemi Vicini Marri
Ludwig Van Beethoven by Richard Tames
Ludwig Van Beethoven by Mike Venezia
Ludwig Van Beethoven: Musical Pioneer by Carol Greene
The Value of Giving: The Story of Beethoven by Ann Donegan Johnson

Language Experience
- How many new words can your students make using the letters in the name *Ludwig Van Beethoven*? See reproducible on page 110.

Writing Experience
- Play music by Beethoven and have students write how the music makes them feel. See reproducible on page 111.

- Let students design a birthday greeting to honor Beethoven on his special day! Have each write a note of thanks to the composer for his music.

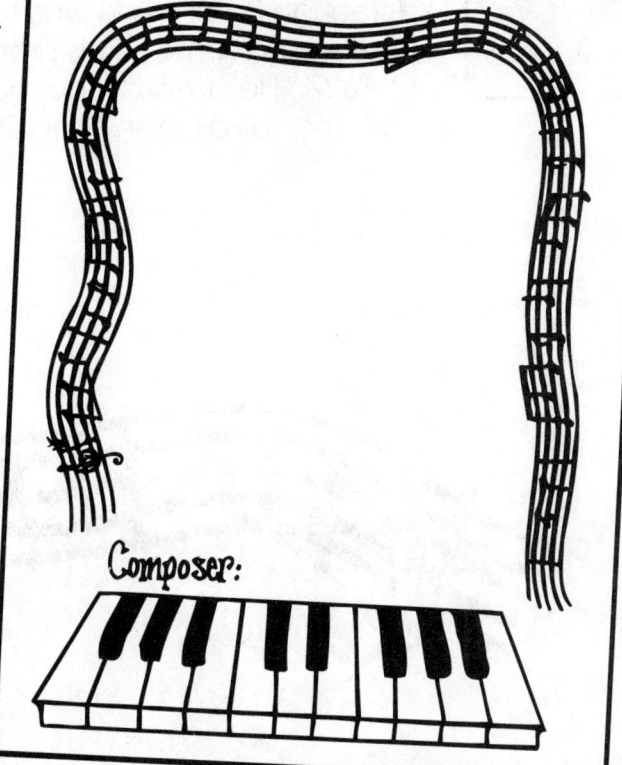

107

Social Studies Experience

- Your students may not be aware that Beethoven was the first major composer to write a symphony with lyrics. Discuss how music has changed over the centuries.

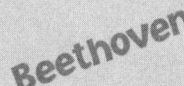

Music/Dramatic Experience

- Have students listen to some of Beethoven's music such as "Moonlight Sonata" or "Ode to Joy."

Physical/Sensory Experience

- Play a game of Musical Chairs to Beethoven's music!

- Although Beethoven was totally deaf before he was 50 years old, he composed some of his greatest music during that time until his death in 1827. He "heard" the music in his head. Challenge students to try reading lips as many hearing impaired people do.

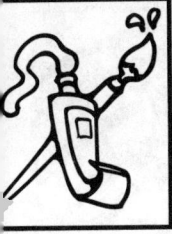

Arts/Crafts Experience

- Let students work on a cooperative art activity while listening to the music of Beethoven. Give each one a sheet of art paper to begin painting or drawing a picture. Every minute or so, stop the music and ask each student to pass his or her art paper to the person on the left. Continue doing this until the pictures are completed.

Beethoven

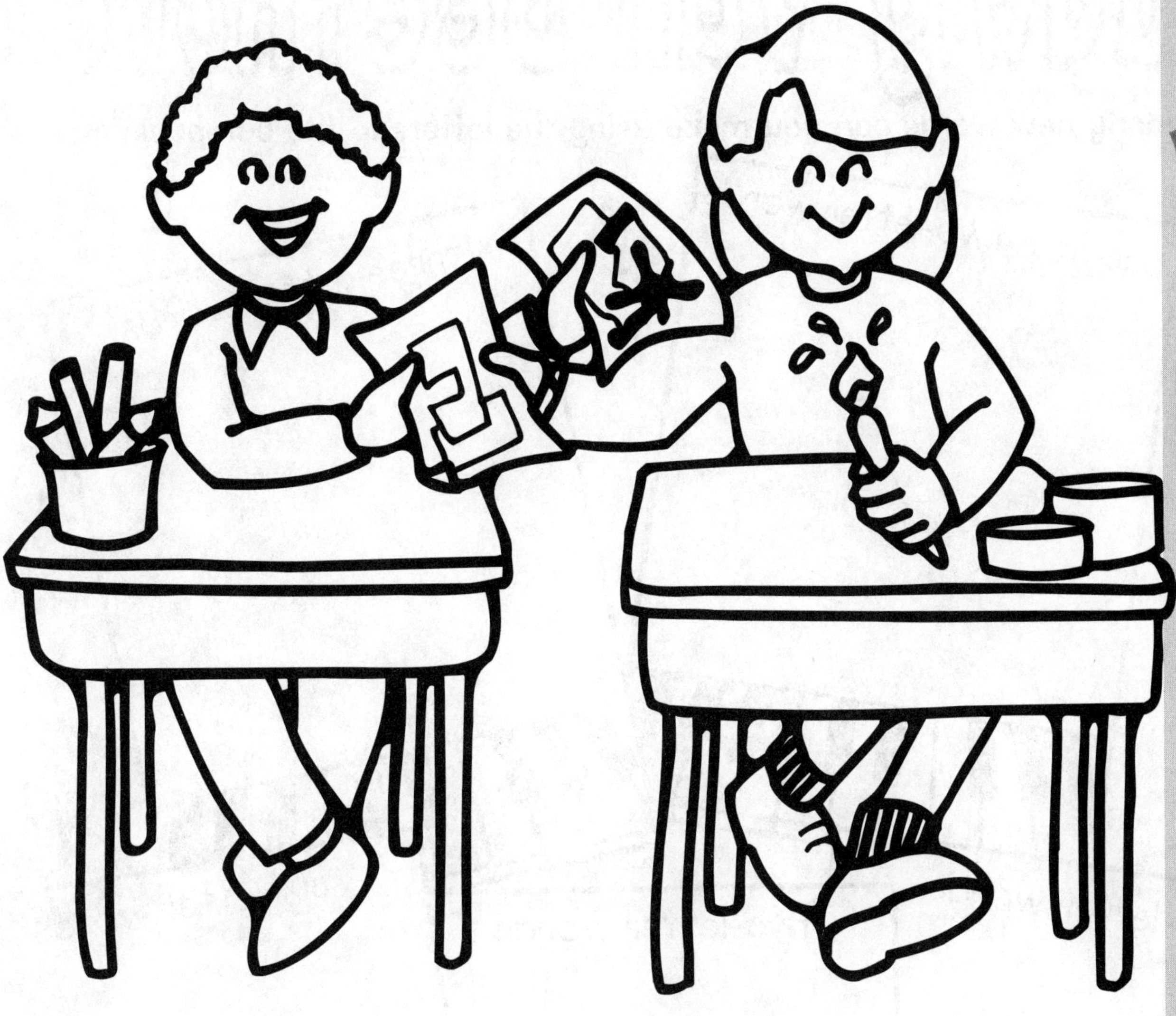

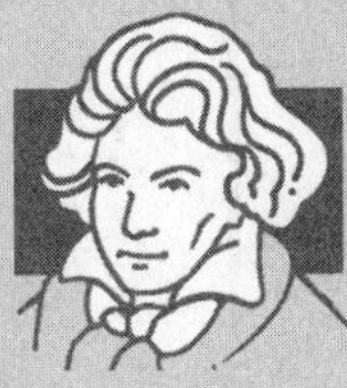

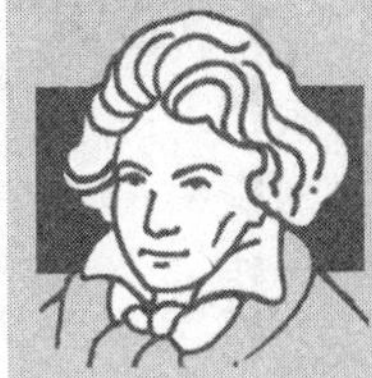

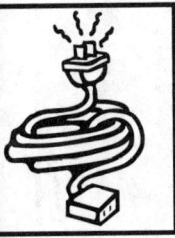

Extension Activities

- Take your class to sit in on a local high school choir practice.

Beethoven

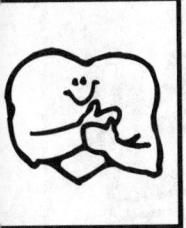

Values Education Experience

- Beethoven was an exceptional musical genius, but we all have talents. Encourage students to use their talents to help other people.

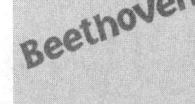

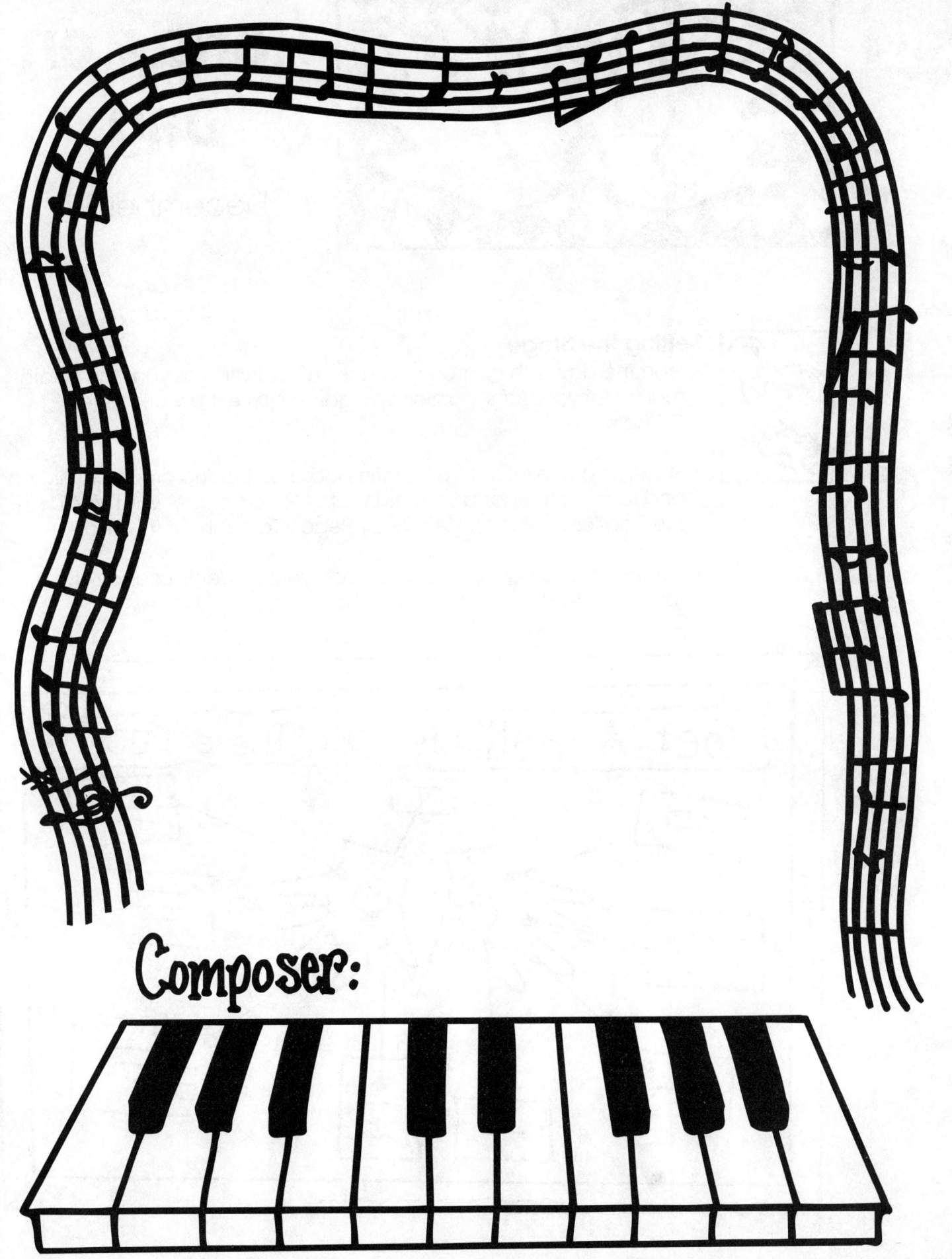

Hands on Day

December 17

Setting the Stage

- Plan the day with as many "hands-on" activities as you can (math manipulative, crafts, puzzles and games) as extra work for fast finishers.

- Students can help with a bulletin board by tracing around their hands and forming the hand shapes into the letters of the word HANDS in the caption: "Joining HANDS for Peace Throughout the Year!"

- Construct a semantic web with facts your students already know (or would like to know) about hands.

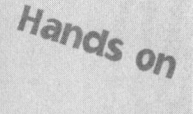

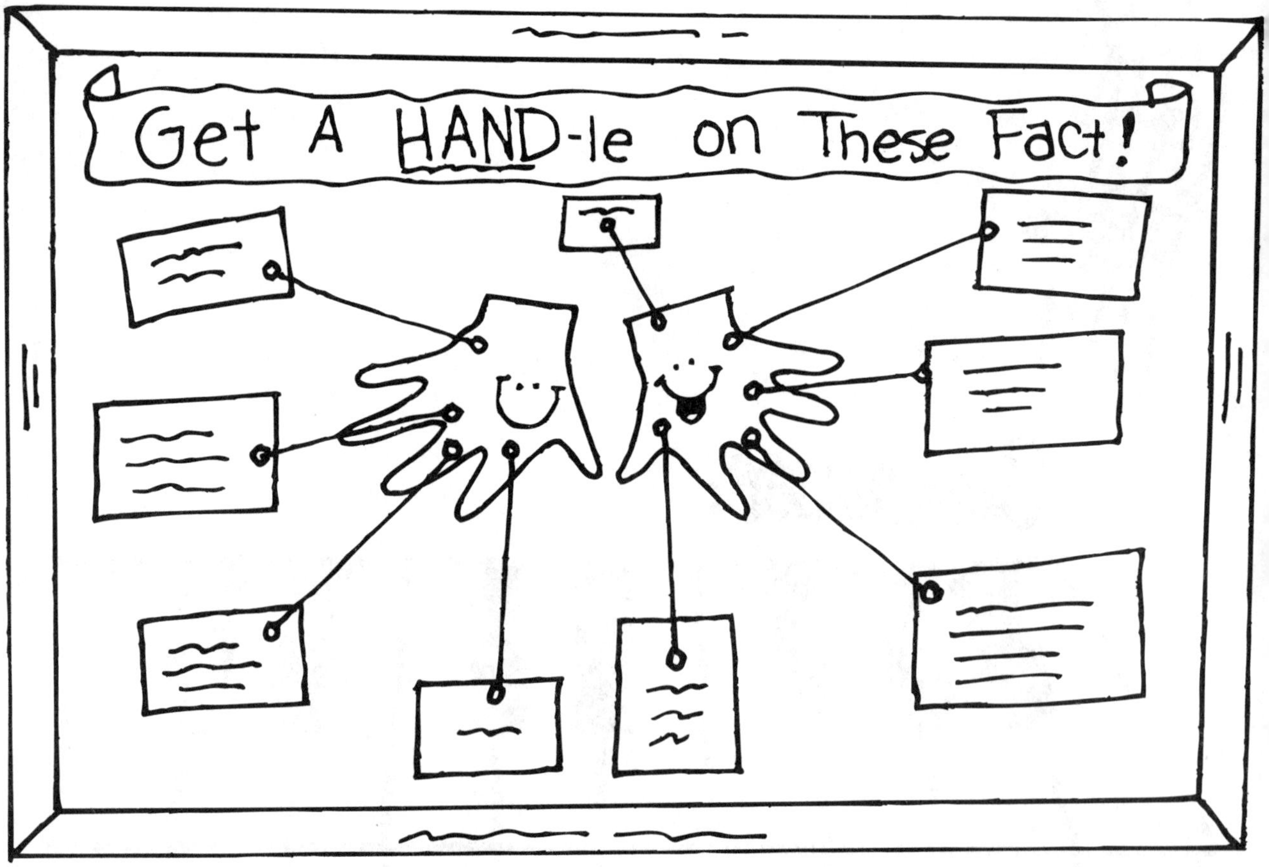

Get A HAND-le on These Fact!

Literary Exploration
A, B, C, D, Tummy, Toes, Hands, Knees by B.G. Hennessy
Clap Your Hands by Lorinda Bryan Cauley
Clap Your Hands: Finger Rhymes by Sarah Hayes and Toni Goffe
Dogs Have Paws by Jan Ross
Do This, Hands! by Nancy Bentley
Feet, Flippers, Hooves and Hands by Mark Rauzon
From Fins to Hands: An Adventure in Evolution by Anthony Ravielli
Hands by Robert James
Hands Off! by Mario Mariotti
Hands Up! by Ruth Goode
The Helping Hands Handbook by Patricia Adams and Jean Marzollo
Here Are My Hands by Bill Martin, et al
Magical Hands by Marjorie Barker
Morgan the Magnificent by Ian Wallace
My Father's Hands by Joanne Ryder
My Hands Can by Jean Holzenthaler
My Hands, My World by Catherine Brighton
Salt Hands by Jane Chelsea Aragon
A Show of Hands: Say It in Sign Language by Mary Beth Sullivan
The Story of Your Hand by Alvin and Virginia Silverstein
The Whole World of Hands by Gilda and Melvin Berger
The Wonder of Hands by Edith Baer
Words in Our Hands by Ada B. Litchfield

Language Experience
- Construct a class Venn diagram depicting the similarities and differences between feet and hands or toes and fingers.

- Challenge students to think of words or phrases that use the word *hand* in them. (Examples: handmade, hands down) Discuss the meaning of each one.

Writing Experience
- Students could write about a time when someone gave them a "hand" and helped them out. See reproducible on page 118.

Math Experience
- Use this day as a chance to work on "hands-on" math manipulatives!
- Play a fun counting game. Choose a student to be the counter at the front of the room. When you say "Hands up," students hold up one or both hands with various fingers up. The counter must quickly count all the fingers. Then another counter takes over until every student has been the counter.

Science/Health Experience
- Reinforce health and safety through cleanliness and germ prevention with a review lesson on the importance of washing hands regularly each day.

Social Studies Experience

- To practice acts of random kindness, institute the "Phantom Hand!" Have a box full of hand shapes available for students. Whenever they see a need for a "helping hand," they can do the job, then leave the mark of the "Phantom Hand" behind. Students will love the mystery of it. It's a great way to encourage anonymous service. See reproducibles on page 119.

Music/Dramatic Experience

- Play a rhythm game of Follow the Leader! The teacher starts out clapping a certain rhythm and students copy it. Then choose a student to be the leader and create his or her own clapping rhythm for others to follow. Let students take turns being the clapping leaders.

- Borrow a sound recording of Sarah Pirtle's "Two Hands Hold the Earth" from your local library. Let students listen to it as they work on school projects today.

- Younger students will enjoy doing finger plays such as "The Eeency Weency Spider."

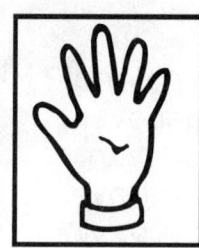

Physical/Sensory Experience

- Let students play the hand game Rock, Paper, Scissors in pairs. A fist stands for rock, an outstretched hand is paper and two fingers criss-crossed designates scissors. Students decide which symbol they will use, then chant together, "Rock, paper, scissors." Depending on which one they choose, only one can be a winner unless they both come up with the same symbol. Rock crushes scissors, paper covers rock and scissors cut paper.

- Teach some sign language! A helpful guide is Mary Beth Sullivan's *A Show of Hands: Say It in Sign Language* or Remy Charlip's *Handtalk: An ABC of Finger Spelling and Signs.*

Arts/Crafts Experience

- Have students make handprints (from paint, ink or clay) to give their parents this holiday season.

- Let students trace their hands on green construction paper several times, cut them out and arrange them in a wreath. A bow at the bottom makes a festive decoration.

Extension Activities

⚠ For a fun and "hand"some treat today, have students fill the fingers of a clear plastic glove (available in medical supply stores) with cooled, popped popcorn. The wrist area can be secured shut with a piece of yarn or rubber band.

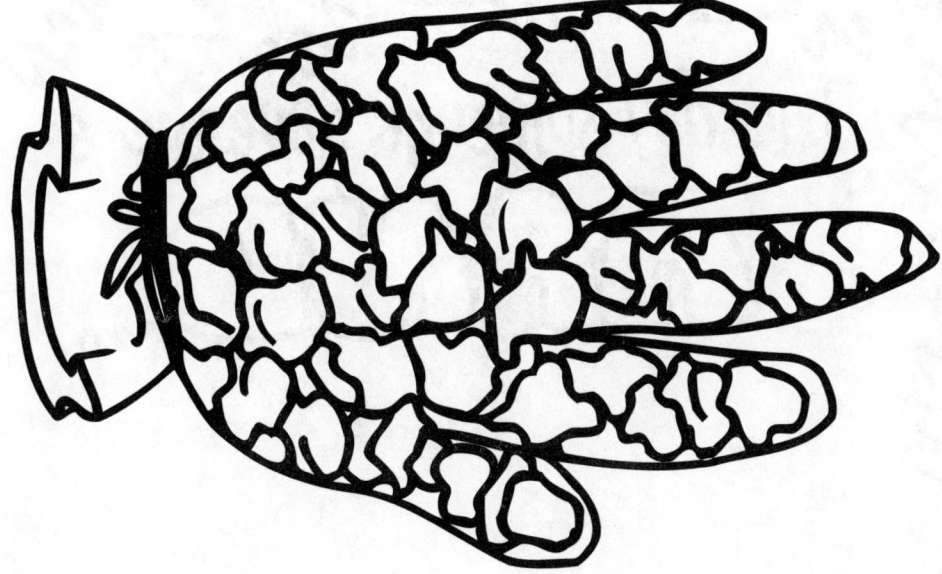

⚠ Serve "finger" sandwiches! Ask students why they think they are called that.

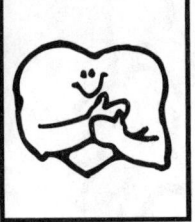

Values Education Experience

• Talk about the value of helpful hands, lifting, creating and soothing rather than grabbing, pushing, hurting.

Nutcracker Day

December 18

Setting the Stage
- Construct a semantic web with facts your students know (or would like to know) about ballet or dance in general.

Historical Background
Peter Tchaikovsky's *Nutcracker* ballet was first performed on this day in St. Petersburg, Russia, in 1892.

Literary Exploration
Favorite Stories of the Ballet by James Riordan
George Balanchine's The Nutcracker by Joel Meyerowitz
Maria Tallchief by Tobi Tobias
The Magic Nutcracker by Margaret Hillert
The Nutcracker by Fiona Black, et al
The Nutcracker by Warren Chappell
The Nutcracker by E.T.A. Hoffman and Rachel Isadora
The Nutcracker by Eduard Petiska
The Nutcracker Ballet by Vladimir Vagin
A Nutcracker in a Tree: A Book of Riddles by Riana Duncan
The Nutcracker Noel by Kate McMullan
The Nutcracker: A Story and a Ballet by Ellen Switzer
Stories from the Classical Ballet by Belinda Hollyer
The Story of the Nutcracker Ballet by Deborah Hautzig
A Very Young Dancer by Jill Krementz

Language Experience

- Read the story to your students, then let your students listen for the main events and characters in the music, *The Nutcracker Suite*. While listening, have them label and illustrate four major scenes from the storyline of *The Nutcracker* on a sheet of paper folded in fourths.

Writing Experience

- Ask students to imagine that a dancer has a sprained ankle the day before his or her ballet debut. Have them write what happens. See reproducible on page 123.

- Students can write about what happens when someone puts on magic shoes. See reproducible on page 124.

Social Studies Experience

- Let interested students research the history of ballet, then share their findings with the rest of the class.

Music/Dramatic Experience

• Let your students listen to Peter Tchaikovsky's *Nutcracker Suite* while they work on holiday projects.

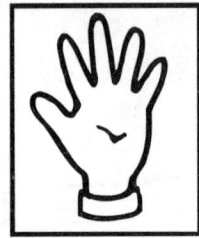

Physical/Sensory Experience

• Get students involved in creative dance and simple movement exercises today. If some of your students are enrolled in dance classes, see if they might be willing to demonstrate a few things for the class.

Arts/Crafts Experience

• As students listen to *The Nutcracker* today, let them draw what they think is happening in the story.

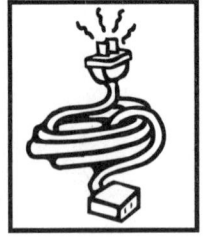

Extension Activities

• Invite a local ballerina or college dance major to visit your class and talk about what he or she does and demonstrate some dance moves.

• Take students on a field trip to see a local dance rehearsal.

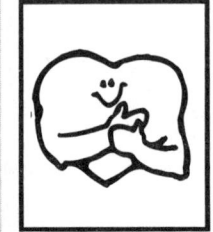

Values Education Experience

• Discuss the value of music and dance. Help your students learn to appreciate the cultural arts.

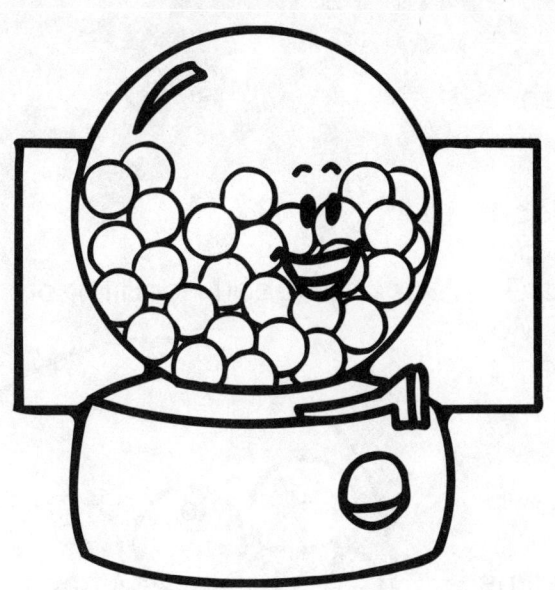

Gumballs Galore Day

December 19

Setting the Stage
- Display various kinds and brands of gum around related literature to get your students excited about the day's activities.

- Construct a semantic web with facts your students know (or would like to know) about gum.

Historical Background
William Semple patented chewing gum in December 1869.

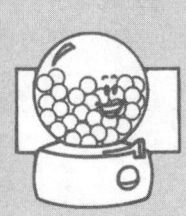

Literary Exploration
Bubble Gum by Gail Jorgensen
Bubble Gum by Kate Noble
Bubble Gum by H.I. Peeples
The Chewing Gum Book by Robert Young
Fun with Gum by Janis Asad Raabe
The Great American Chewing Gum Book by Robert Hendrickson
Just a Gum Wrapper by Gina Mayer
Mr. Bubble Gum by William Hooks

Language Experience
- Have students color a gumball machine, then glue round, colorful gumballs in it every time they succeed at a new skill—letter recognition, high-frequency words, multiplication tables and so on. They can write the skills on the balls. See reproducibles on pages 129-130.

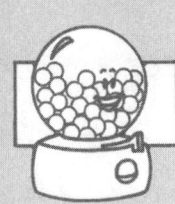

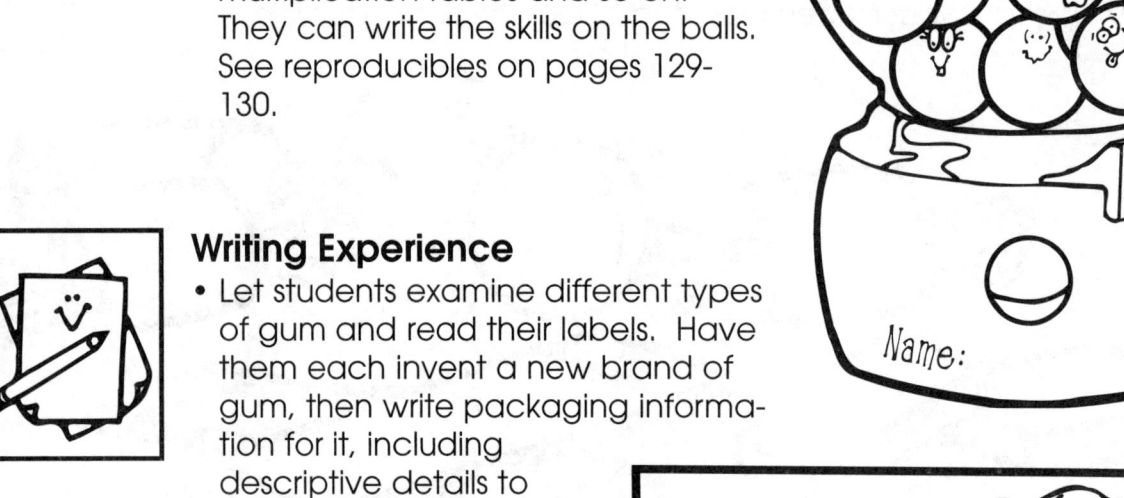

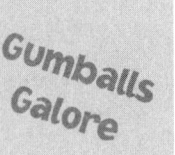

Writing Experience
- Let students examine different types of gum and read their labels. Have them each invent a new brand of gum, then write packaging information for it, including descriptive details to promote sales as well as a list of ingredients.

- Leave some gumball-shaped story starters at a writing center with ideas such as: "You'll never believe it, but I blew such a big bubble that . . ." See reproducible on page 131.

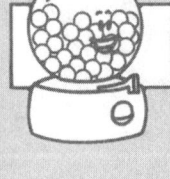

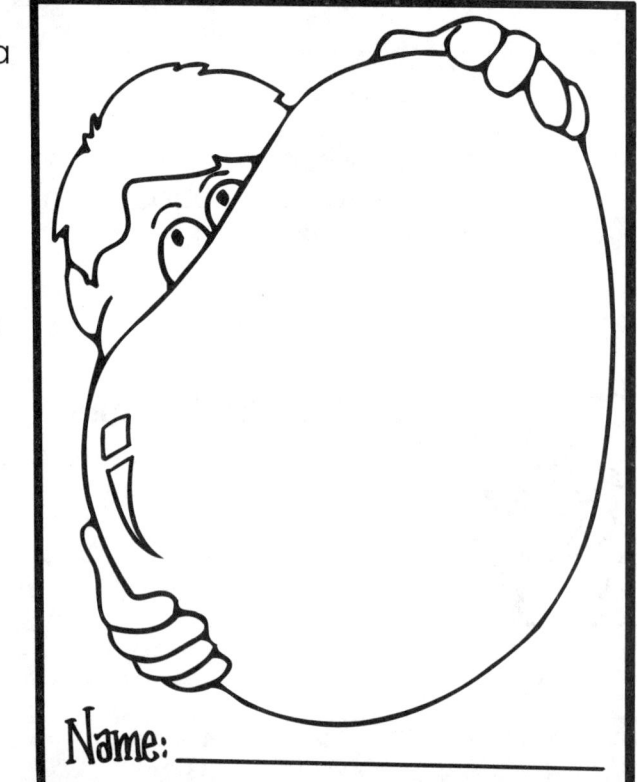

Math Experience
- Get your students involved in gum graphing! They can graph various types of gum showing color, shape, size and flavor.

Science/Health Experience
- Let interested students research how chewing gum is made, then share the information with the class.

Social Studies Experience
- Explain to students that people have been chewing gum for centuries in South America. They chewed sap from trees such as the sapodilla tree or leaves or wads of grass to get that same "chewing gum" sensation. Let interested students do additional research and share their findings with the rest of the class.

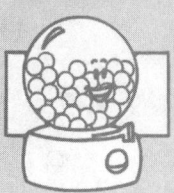
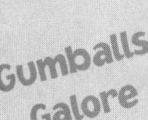

Gumballs Galore

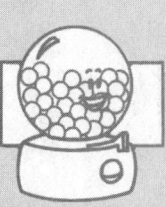
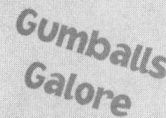

Gumballs Galore

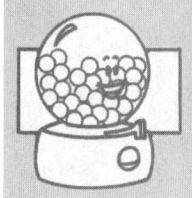

Gumballs Galore

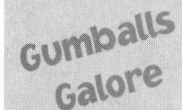

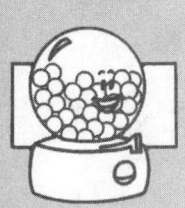 

Music/Dramatic Experience

- Let students debate the issue of whether or not chewing gum should be allowed in school. Each side needs to defend their opinion with good reasons.

- Borrow Rich Charette's sound recording of *Mr. Bubble Gum and Other Songs for Hungry Kids* from a local library and play it for your students while they work on holiday projects.

Gumballs Galore

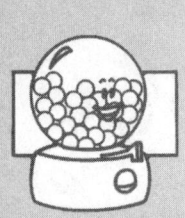 

Physical/Sensory Experience

⚠ Host a Bubble Gum Blowing Contest! Give each student a couple pieces of sugar-free bubble gum. Let everyone blow three bubbles. The largest bubble wins the contest.

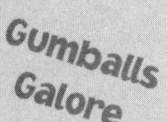

Gumballs Galore

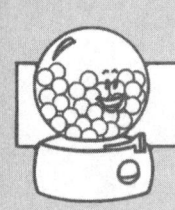

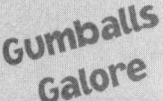

Gumballs Galore

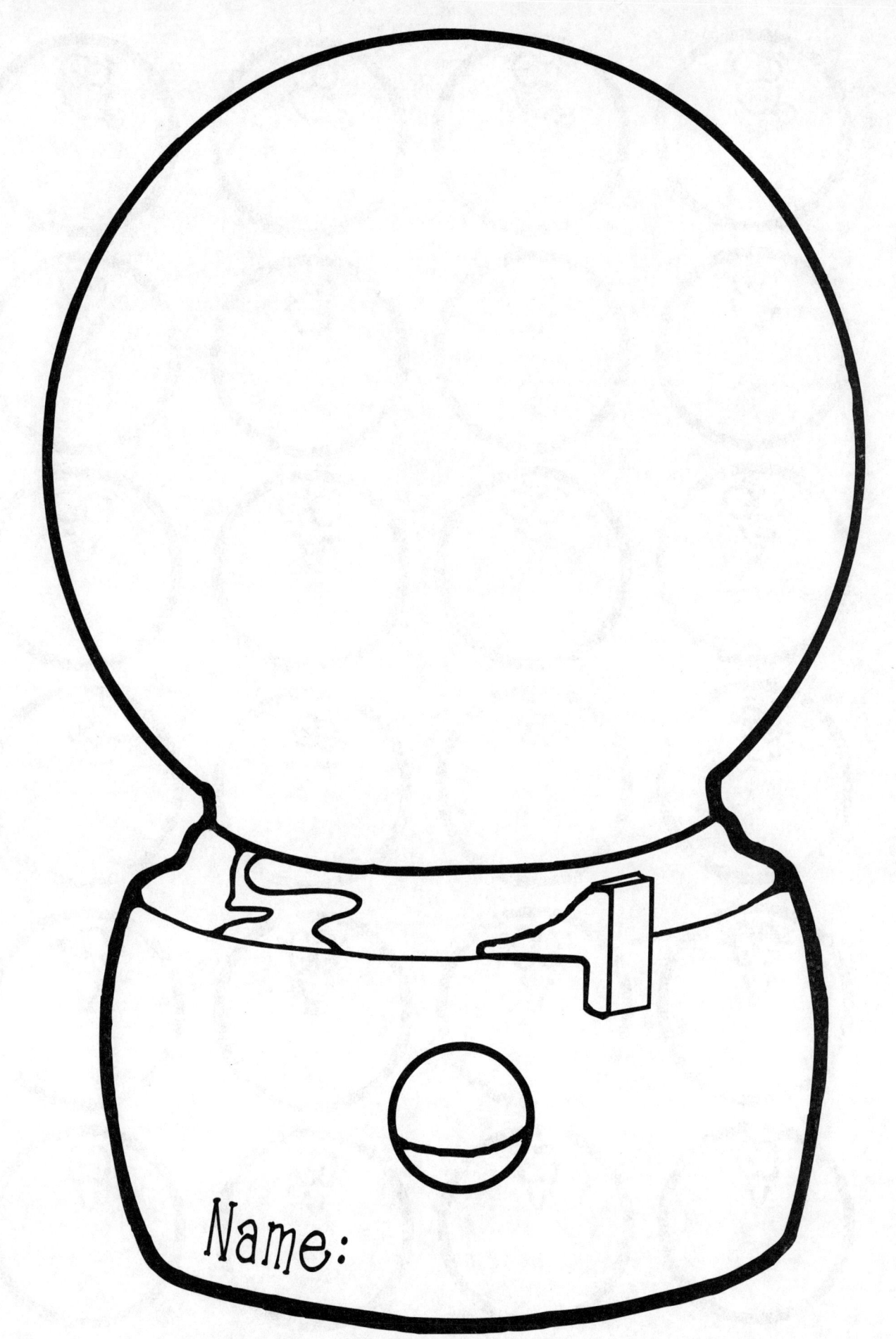

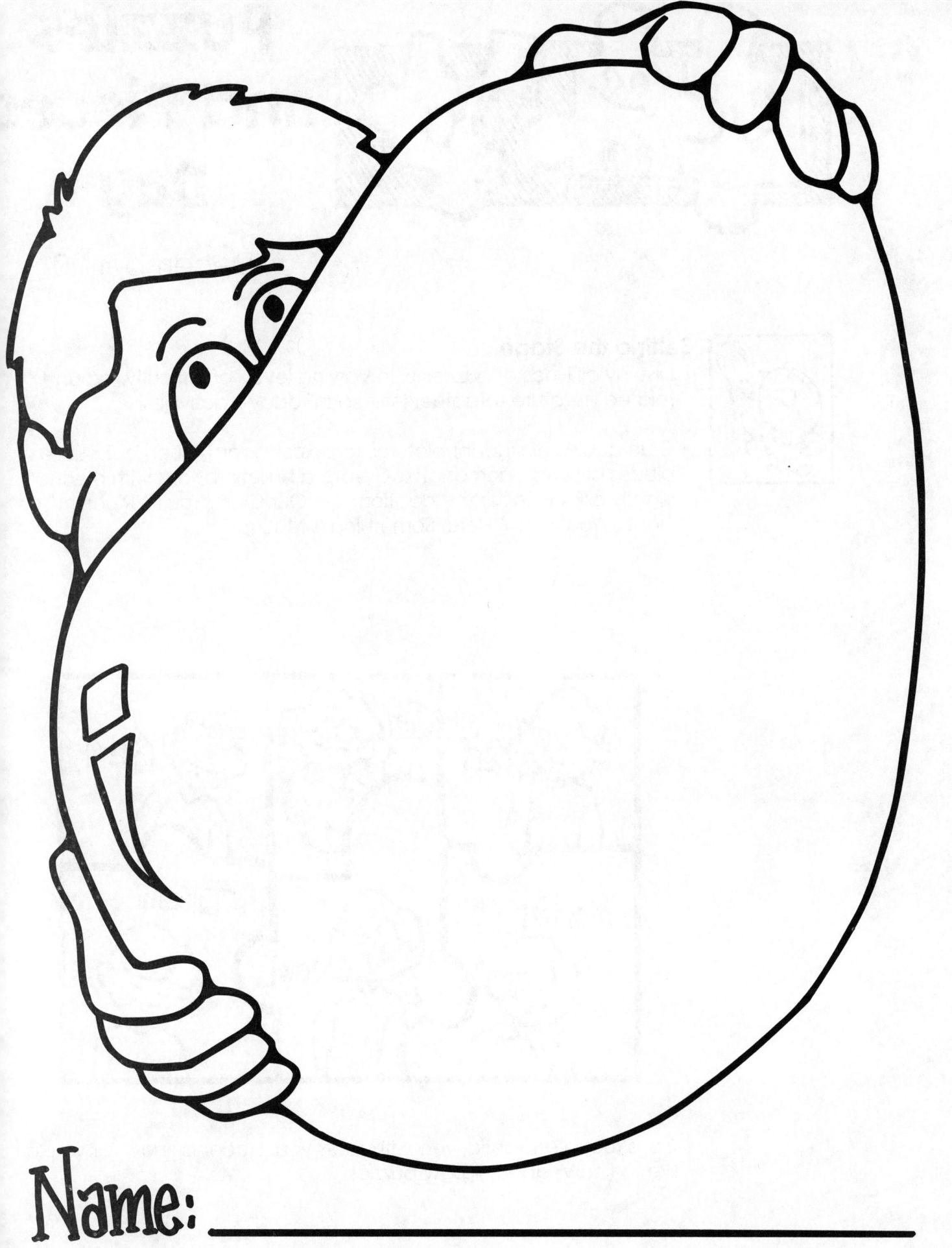

Name: _____

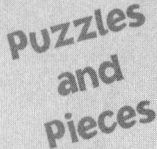

Puzzles and Pieces Day

December 20

Setting the Stage

- Display all kinds of puzzles with varying levels of difficulty, around related literature to gather interest in today's activities.

- Glue copies of student pictures to poster board. Then cut puzzle pieces around each photo. Create a bulletin board with pieces slightly askew under the caption: "In Our Class, You Fit Right In!" or "When You're Not Here, Something Is Missing!"

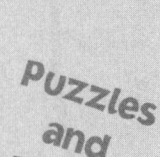

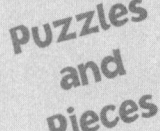

- Construct a semantic web with facts your students know (or would like to know) about jigsaw puzzles.

Historical Background
John Spilsbury created the first jigsaw puzzle as a tool to help students reinforce their geography skills. Those first puzzle pieces were carved out of wood and hand painted.

Literary Exploration
Eye Count: A Book of Counting Puzzles by Linda Bourke
My First Book of Puzzles by Charlotte Knox
Pick a Peck of Puzzles by Arnold Roth
Pigs from 1 to 10 by Arthur Geisert
Puzzles by Brian Wildsmith

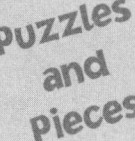

Writing Experience
- Use a puzzle as a springboard for writing! Students complete simple puzzles, then write stories about them.

Physical/Sensory Experience
- Let students draw pictures or cut out magazine pictures to create puzzles. They may exchange puzzles with a friend and solve each other's.

- Using the puzzle pattern on page 135, students can glue a picture on the back, then cut out the puzzle pieces. Provide envelopes for students to store the puzzle pieces in.

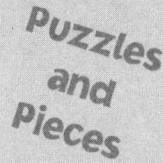

Arts/Crafts Experience

• Let students make Rudolph the Red-Nosed Reindeer pins from puzzle Give each student three jigsaw puzzle pieces. They paint them with brown tempera paint and let them dry. Then they arrange the puzzle pieces so that one piece is Rudolph's head and the other two are hi antlers. They glue on two large, wiggly eyes and a red pom-pom nose with craft glue. A pin clasp (found in craft stores) can be glued to the back for a final touch! This can be a fun holiday gift for Mom.

• Give each student one puzzle piece. Have them imagine and draw what they think the rest of the puzzle looks like.

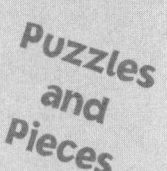

Extension Activities

• Ask students ahead of time to bring their favorite puzzles from home so you can have a puzzle marathon!

• Make a giant puzzle with the class' cooperative effort. Cut a very large piece of butcher paper into giant puzzle pieces. Students each glue a piece of it to light cardboard (such as from a cereal box). Students can paint their pictures on their puzzle pieces. Then they can start assembling the giant puzzle together.

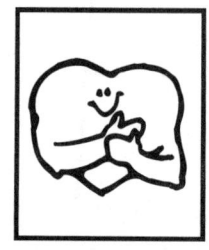

Values Education Experience

• Discuss the ways in which every individual is like a piece of a puzzle. When students understand this concept, they will be more likely to accept and appreciate other students.

Crossword Puzzle Day

December 21

Setting the Stage

- On a bulletin board display a variety of crossword puzzles with the caption: "Sometimes School Is Puzzling!" Display crossword puzzle books next to the display. Advise students that when they get their classwork done, they can select puzzles to solve.

- Construct a semantic web with facts your students know (or would like to know) about crossword puzzles.

Historical Background

On this day in 1913, the first crossword puzzle was published in the *New York World* newspaper.

Literary Exploration

Test Your Wits by Sheila Anne Barry
Word Bird Makes Words with Hen by Jane Belk Moncure

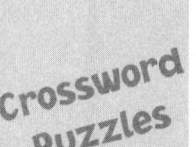

Language Experience

- Prepare students for working crossword puzzles today by testing their vocabulary. Print the following words on the board and challenge them to come up with two or more synonyms for each one: *bright, small, large, often, good, bad, test, thin.*

- Let each student write five words on a sheet of paper, then pass the paper to the student on his or her right. Students must write a synonym for each word on the page, then pass the paper on to the next student in line. Pass the papers four or five times, then return them to their owners to read.

Writing Experience

- Challenge students to write mystery stories about a newspaper writer who gives clues to the crimes he commits in crossword puzzles. Can the police figure out his clues and catch him before he strikes again?

- Have students write acrostic poems about puzzles. Every word they come up with must begin with one of the letters in the word *puzzle*. The poems do not need to rhyme.

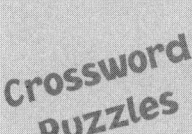

Math Experience

- Create a cross-number puzzle for students to solve. Give math problems or questions for students to answer with numbers instead of words. (Example: 2 Down = the number of days in a year.) Give each student a copy of your number puzzle to solve or copy the one on page 139. When the puzzles are done, check the answers.

- Check out Sudoku, the number puzzle from Japan.

Science/Health Experience

- Explain that research and experiments on the human brain have shown that one good way to stay mentally alert and exercise one's thinking and reasoning abilities is to work on puzzles. Crossword puzzles are good, but there are also many other kinds of puzzles we can enjoy: word searches, cryptograms, acrostics, logic puzzles, etc. Ask students what their favorite kinds of puzzles are. Encourage them to keep their brains active by working on puzzles and even making up their own puzzles to solve. (Example: Instead of just sitting in the car at the railroad tracks waiting for a train to go by, count the cars.)

Social Studies Experience

- Create a crossword puzzle on states or countries for students to solve. (Example: 3 Across = Hollywood state.) Give each student a copy of your crossword puzzle or copy the one on page 139. (Answers included on page 190.) When the puzzles are done, check the answers together.

- Challenge each student to create a crossword puzzle about himself or herself. The words used may include: *father, mother, house, cat, brother,* etc. Clues should be the names of the people, the family pet, etc. When the puzzles are done, students may give them to someone else to solve. Each student will receive someone else's puzzle. This is not only a good way to help students think clearly and logically, but it also helps them get to know more about the other students in their class.

Music/Dramatic Experience
- Let students work on crossword puzzles as they listen to classical or holiday music.

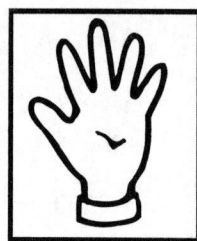

Physical/Sensory Experience
- Use masking tape to make a tic-tac-toe board on the floor. Make X and O signs for students to hold. Divide students into two teams, Xs and Os. Ask questions to review math concepts or to review what they have been learning in science and social studies. If a student answers a question correctly, he or she goes to stand on the tic-tac-toe board in the best square possible. The player on the opposing team is then asked a question and if he or she answers correctly, goes to stand on another square. The teams try to get three in a row or block each other from getting three in a row.

Arts/Crafts Experience
- Let students draw pictures on cardstock of themselves and their friends or family playing their favorite games. Then have them cut each picture into about 10 puzzle pieces. Provide envelopes in which they can store the puzzle pieces. They can exchange puzzles with one another to put them together, then take their puzzles home for their families to put together.

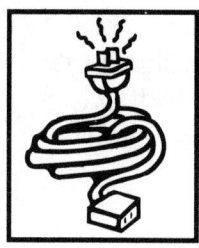

Extension Activities
- Let students work together in small groups to create crossword puzzles, then copy them and put them in packets to take to an area adult care center. Remind them that some senior citizens don't see well, so the puzzle boxes and clues should be larger and easy to read. If possible, take the class to visit a care center so they can personally give their puzzles to the residents.

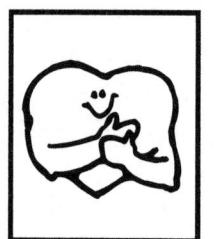

Values Education Experience
- Ask students what it takes to solve a difficult puzzle (patience, persistence, focus). Discuss how these are not only important character traits for doing puzzles, but for everyday life.

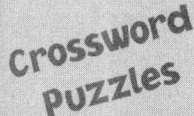

Follow-Up/Homework Idea
- Have students take home the puzzles they created and challenge their families to solve them.

State the State Crossword Puzzle

Across
1. To the right of Minnesota
4. Between Oregon and Canada
8. Lone Star state of cowboys
9. Home of Chicago

Down
2. Between Washington and California
3. Home of Las Vegas
5. Biggest state
6. Home of Indianapolis Speedway
7. Birthplace of Presidents Van Buren, Filmore and both Roosevelts
10. To the right of Indiana

Cross-Number Puzzle

Across
3. Inches in two feet
4. 2602 - 1000
5. 31 + 13
6. 1000 x 2 + 1
7. Minutes in four hours

Downs
1. Days in a year
2. 111 + 111
3. Two dozen
5. 525 - 113

Cloud Nine Day

December 22

Setting the Stage
- Attach balls of cotton and lace doilies to dental floss and suspend them from the ceiling. Also hang toy airplanes and balloons. You might even want to buy cotton batting to place here and there as if the class were walking in the clouds today.

- Construct a semantic map or web with facts your students know about clouds. Then let them list questions they have about clouds to help you structure the day's activities.

Literary Exploration

Bailey's Window by Kinuko Craft
Bartholomew and the Oobleck by Dr. Suess
The Cloud Book by Tomie de Paola
Cloud Eyes by Kathryn Lasky
Cloud Nine by Norman Silver
Cloud over Clarence by Marc Brown
C.L.O.U.D.S. by Pat Cummings
Cloudy with a Chance of Meatballs by Judi Barrett
Exploring the Sky by Day by Terence Dickinson
Eyewitness Books: Weather by Brian Cosgrove
Eyewitness Explorers: Weather by John Farndon and John Bendall-Brunello
It Looked Like Spilt Milk by Charles G. Shaw
Jonathan's Cloud by Gardner McFall
Little Cloud by Eric Carle
Poofin: The Cloud That Cried on Christmas by Richard Wainwright
Small Cloud by Ariane
Storms by Seymour Simon
Weather and Forecasting by Storm Dunlop and Francis Wilson
The Weather Sky by Bruce McMillan

Language Experience

- Discuss figures of speech using the word *cloud* such as: "walking on cloud nine" or "someone's got his head in the clouds."

- Provide students with a handful of Q-tips™. Have them lay down the Q-tips™ to spell words, creating a "skywriting" look.

Writing Experience

- Students can write letters with their questions or comments and ask for cloud pamphlets or charts at:

  WEATHERWORKS
  1522 Baylor Ave.
  Rockville, MD 20850

- Explain that some days are cloud watching, lazy days for daydreaming. Provide cloud shapes on which students can write about their daydreams. Hang the cloud writing from the ceiling with dental floss or fishing line. See reproducible on page 146.

- Read about "Cloudmen" in the book *James and the Giant Peach* by Roald Dahl (beginning with chapter 27). Let students write additional adventures for the "Cloudmen."

- If it is a nice day, have students stretch out on the school lawn and watch the clouds. Have them write adventures about figures or shapes they see in the clouds.

- Have students imagine that a cloud comes low to the ground and actually picks them up, carrying them into the sky. Let them write what happens. See reproducible on page 147.

Math Experience
- Students can make and match cloud shape problems with their cloud shape answer counterparts and then exchange with others in the class. See reproducible on page 148.

Science/Health Experience
- Examine how clouds form through this experiment. Fill a two-liter plastic soda bottle with very warm water, about 3/4 full. Light a match and drop it into the bottle, as you quickly put the bottle cap on. Let a student apply pressure to the sides of the bottle by squeezing it, then letting it go. After the bottle is squeezed, a small cloud-like form should appear inside the bottle because the warm air moisture condenses when it comes in contact with cold air. Clouds are formed when all these tiny droplets in the air meet warmer air.

Science/Health Experience continued

- Study different kinds of cloud formations. Define each cloud term: *stratus*—"stretched out," *cumulus*—"pile," *cirrus*—"curl" and *nimbus*—"rain." Let students paint with white tempera on dark construction paper to make these different formations.

- Go outside together to study cloud formations. Let students make observational drawings. Have them divide papers into four sections. Take the class out several times to see how the clouds change throughout the day. Students should draw the changes they see.

Music/Dramatic Experience

- Play different types of music as students dance like fluffy clouds, rain clouds and storm clouds.

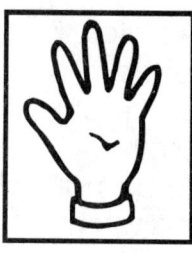

Physical/Sensory Experience

⚠ Let students finger-paint with cooled instant mashed potato "clouds" on wax paper. Shaving cream can be substituted.

- Give each student a "cloud," a white blown-up balloon tied to the ankle. Tell them to protect it from "lightning storms." Choose students to be lightning trying to burst the "cloud" balloons with plastic spoons. Students run away from the "lightning" to protect their clouds. The last student with a cloud intact is "King or Queen Cloud!"

Arts/Crafts Experience

- Students can cut cloud shapes from wax paper to display on class windows for a little indoor "weather watching."

- Give each students two pieces of cheesecloth or white cotton fabric. Let them cut matching cloud shapes and sew them together, leaving a small opening. They can stuff cotton batting into the opening before sewing it closed. These fabric clouds can be suspended from the ceiling or used at the class reading area.

Cloud nine

Extension Activities

⚠ Did you ever eat a cloud? Let students add mini marshmallows to whipped topping, freeze it for about an hour, then enjoy it.

⚠ After reading, *Cloudy with a Chance of Meatballs* by Judi Barrett to the students, involve them in these activities: illustrate the sequence of events in the story; write their feelings about the food choices given; fry meatballs in an electric skillet. Skewer meatballs with toothpicks to serve to students.

Cloud nine

Cloud nine

Follow-Up/Homework Idea

- Instruct students to observe the clouds before sunset and make an observational drawing to show their parents.

Japanese Emperor's Birthday

December 23

Setting the Stage
- Mount a map of Japan on a bulletin board. Around the map place pictures from travel magazines of life in Japan or a poster of Japan from a travel agency.

- Construct a semantic web with facts your students know (or would like to know) about Japan.

Historical Background
On this day in 1933, Japanese Emperor Akihito was born. This is a holiday in Japan to honor the nation's leader.

Literary Exploration
The Dancing Kettle and Other Japanese Folk Tales by Yoshilo Uchida and Richard Jones
Japan by Ann Heinrichs
Japan by Susan McKay
Sam Samurai by Jon Schieszka
Screen of Frogs: An Old Tale by Sheila Hamanake
Sophie and the Rising Sun by Augusta Trobaugh
Three Strong Women: A Tall Tale from Japan by Claus Stamm
Two Foolish Cats by Yoskiko Uchida

Language Experience
- Tell students that the Japanese call their country *Nippon* which means "source of the sun." Challenge them to find out the names of other countries and their meanings. (Example: Germany is called Deutschland by the German people.)

Language Experience continued

- Your students will enjoy learning these Japanese words:

yes	hai (HAH-ee)
no	iie (ee-EH)
thank you	domo arigato (DOH-mo ah-REE-gah-toh)
good morning	ahayo gozaimasu (oh-HAH-yo go-ZAH-ee-mahs)
good-bye	sayonara (sah-YO-nah-rah)

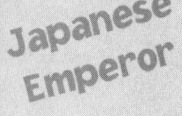

Writing Experience

- Students in Japan go to school Monday through Friday, but they also attend school a half day on Saturday. And their summer vacation time is only for six weeks. Have students write essays expressing their feelings about which is the better school schedule—Japan's or theirs. Have them give good reasons for their opinions.

- Puppet theater is very popular in Japan. Let students work in pairs to write puppet scripts to act out, using the stick puppets they will make from the patterns on page 152. Encourage them to be creative and humorous. See instructions on page 151.

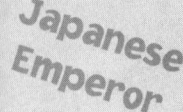

Math Experience

- The population of Japan is 128 million (2003 census). Print the number on the board and have students read it aloud together. Have them find out the population of the United States and figure out the difference in the two numbers. Which country has more people? Compare Japan's population with that of other countries.

Science/Health Experience

- Japan is famous for the electronic equipment they manufacture as well as cars and office machinery. Take students on a brief walk around the school parking lot to check out the parked cars. How many can they find that are Japanese? (Toyota, Nissan, Honda, Mitsubishi, etc.)

Social Studies Experience

- Have students find Japan on a world map. Have them count the number of islands that make up Japan. (They'll probably only count the four large ones, but there are thousands of small islands, too.)

- Let students each make a Japanese flag by cutting a large circle from red fabric and gluing it at the center of a rectangle of white fabric. They can fold the left side of the flag over a drinking straw and glue it down for a flagpole.

Music/Dramatic Experience

- Play a cassette or CD of Japanese music for students to listen to. Talk about how it sounds different from American music.

- Karaoke is a Japanese form of entertainment that has become popular in the United States. Play some familiar music and let volunteers sing solos or duets to entertain the rest of the class.

Physical/Sensory Experience

⚠ Bring a rice dish to class and let students try eating it with chopsticks. Explain that in Japan children begin learning how to eat with chopsticks at the same age children in other countries learn to use a spoon. Remind them that they must hold the chopsticks in just one hand.

Arts/Crafts Experience

- The Japanese teach their children origami (paper folding) at home and in school. Check out a book on origami and help students make a basic origami pattern such as a bird, fish or frog.

- Calligraphy is another popular art in Japan. Artists use a paintbrush and black ink to draw Japanese symbols on paper with simple strokes. Let students come up with their own symbols and paint them on art paper in calligraphy style.

- Have students make puppets by coloring and cutting out the patterns on page 152. Then they can glue a tongue depressor to the back of each pattern to make a stick puppet. They can use their puppets to act out skits they have written. See page 150.

Values Education Experience

- In Japan respect for the elderly is very important. Discuss how students can show respect and honor for their grandparents and elderly neighbors.

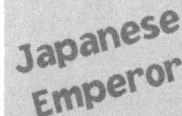

Follow-Up/Homework Idea

- Have students go home and get permission from their parents to eat a traditional meal of rice, fish and tea, or go to a Japanese restaurant for an authentic meal. Everyone should try to eat at least some of the meal with chopsticks.

Christmas Eve Day

December 24

Setting the Stage
- Display Christmas symbols: tree, ornaments, Santa Claus, gifts, wreaths, angels, stars, etc., around the room.

- Construct a semantic web with facts your students know (or would like to know) about Christmas.

Historical Background
December 24th is set aside as Christmas Eve for Christians around the world, the night before the biggest holiday celebrated in many countries.

Literary Exploration
Amahl and the Night Visitors by Gian-Carlo Menotti
The Animals Came First by Jean Louise Welch
A Certain Small Shepherd by Rebecca Caudill
Christmas Eve by Sucie Stevenson
A Christmas Eve Alphabet by Carole Gerber
Christmas Eve at Santa's by Alf Proysen, et al
Little Critters the Night Before Christmas by Mercer Mayer
Madeline's Christmas by Ludwig Bemelmans
Miss Flora McFlimsey's Christmas Eve by Mariana
Mousekin's Christmas Eve by Edna Miller
The Night Before Christmas by Clement C. Moore
On Christmas Eve by Margaret Wise Brown
On Christmas Eve by Peter Collington
Prairie Night Before Christmas by James Rice
Twas the Night Before Christmas by Fred Waring

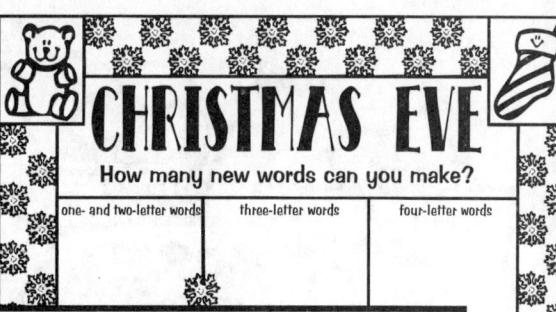

Language Experience
- How many new words can your students make using the letters in *Christmas Eve*? See reproducible on page 155.

Writing Experience
- Have students write about their feelings on the night before Christmas. See reproducible on page 156.

- Have students write invitations to Santa to have him come to their houses for Christmas dinner.

Music/Dramatic Experience
- Students can act out the events as told in "The Night Before Christmas," by Clement C. Moore.

- Sing Christmas songs. Let students choose their favorites.

Arts/Crafts Experience
- Let students draw scenes of Christmas Eve in a variety of places: a mall, someone's home, the North Pole, a church or a hospital.

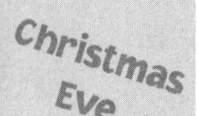

Follow-Up/Homework Idea
- Leave cookies and milk for Santa and carrots and grass for his reindeer.

Christmas Eve Feelings

Christmas Day
December 25

Setting the Stage
- Construct a semantic web with facts your students know (or would like to know) about Christmas.

- Mount a large gift wrapped box top on a bulletin board. Leave the bottom free to be lifted up. Under the package mount a sign that says: "Have a Very Merry Christmas!" Students can lift up (open) the package to read the greeting.

Historical Background
December 25th is the official Christmas Day for Christians everywhere. It began as a religious celebration, but is now also observed as a secular holiday by many people in the world.

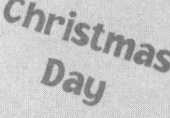

Literary Exploration
At Christmas Be Merry: Verses by R.K. Roche
Christmas Day in the Morning by Pearl Buck
Merry Christmas from Eddie by Carolyn Haywood
Merry Christmas, Little Critter! by Mercer Mayer
Merry Christmas, Mom and Dad by Mercer Mayer
Merry Christmas, Amelia Bedelia by Peggy Parish
We Wish You a Merry Christmas by Tracey Campbell Pearson

Writing Experience

- Students can write what they love about giving at Christmas. See reproducible on page 160.

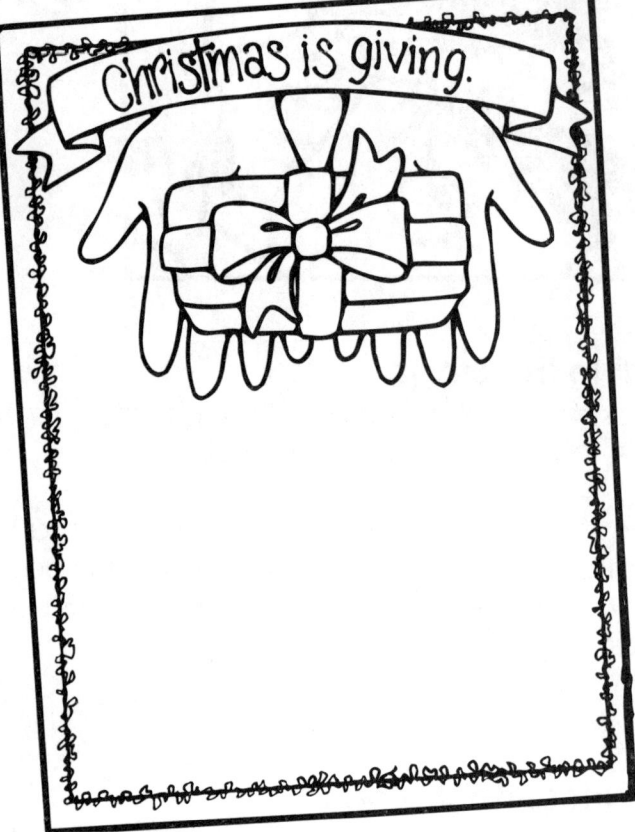

- Students can write about Christmas morning. Was it as they hoped? What happened?

Music/Dramatic Experience

- Sing "Have Yourself a Merry Little Christmas" (words and music by Hugh Martin and Ralph Blane) or the traditional favorite "We Wish You a Merry Christmas."

Physical/Sensory Experience

- Host a Christmas Cleanup Contest. Have student teams compete to see who can do the best job of cleaning up the classroom in a specified time.

Arts/Crafts Experience

- Let students draw a comic strip to illustrate Christmas Day at their house.

- Have students make thank-you cards to send to those who gave them Christmas gifts. See patterns for card and envelope on page 161.

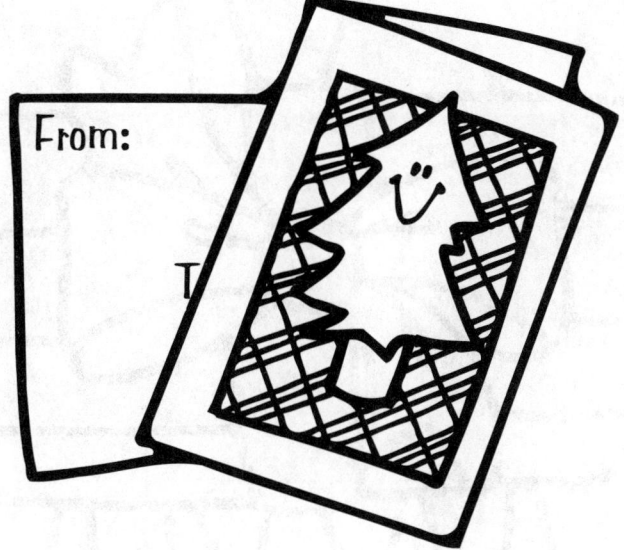

Extension Activities

- Host a silly Christmas dinner. Give the food alternative names: whipped potatoes—"snowflakes," fruit cobbler—"rum pum pum," roast turkey—"angel wings," vegetables or salad—"mistletoe" and cranberries—"holly and berries." Let students sign up for items by their alternative names. They'll be surprised to see what they end up with!

Values Education Experience

- Let volunteers share their feelings about what Christmas means to them.

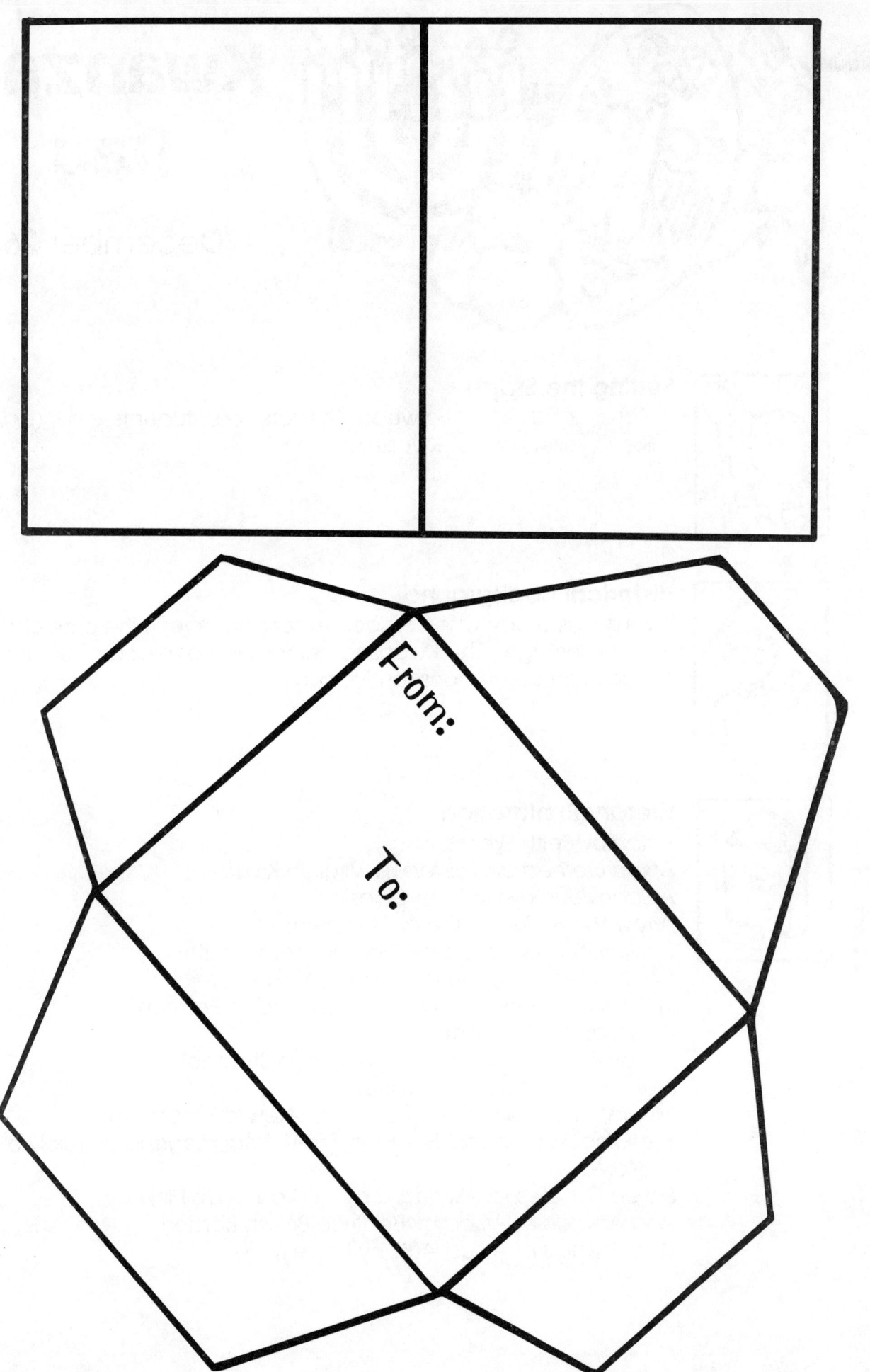

Kwanzaa Day
December 26

Setting the Stage
- Construct a semantic web with facts your students know (or would like to know) about Kwanzaa.

Historical Background
Kwanzaa is a day when African Americans everywhere celebrate their African heritage. The Kwanzaa celebration begins on December 26th and lasts for seven consecutive days.

Literary Exploration
Africa by Keith Lye
Africa Brothers and Sisters by Virginia Kroll
African Journey by John Chiasson
Arrow to the Sun by Gerald McDermott
Celebrating Kwanzaa by Dian Hoyt-Goldsmith
Doctor De Soto Goes to Africa by William Steig
Imani's Gift at Kwanzaa by Denise Burden-Patmon
Kwanzaa by A.P. Porter
Mufaro's Beautiful Daughters by John Steptoe
Music of Africa by Fred Warren
My First Kwanzaa Book by Deborah Newton Chocolate
The Princess Who Lost Her Hair: An Akamba Legend by Tololwa M. Mollel
Seven Candles for Kwanzaa by Andrea Davis Pinkney
Wild Animals of Africa by Beatrice Brown Borden
Wild Animals of Africa ABC by Hope Ryden

Language Experience
- Discuss the literary genre of African folktales. Read aloud an example such as: *The Princess Who Lost Her Hair: An Akamba Legend* retold by Tololwa M. Mollel

Science/Health Experience
- Let interested students research animals found in Africa, then share their findings with the rest of the class.

Social Studies Experience
- Show students the continent of Africa on a world map or globe. Talk about the climate in the various areas and the diverse groups of people found in them. Let interested students do additional research on the continent, then share their findings with the rest of the class.

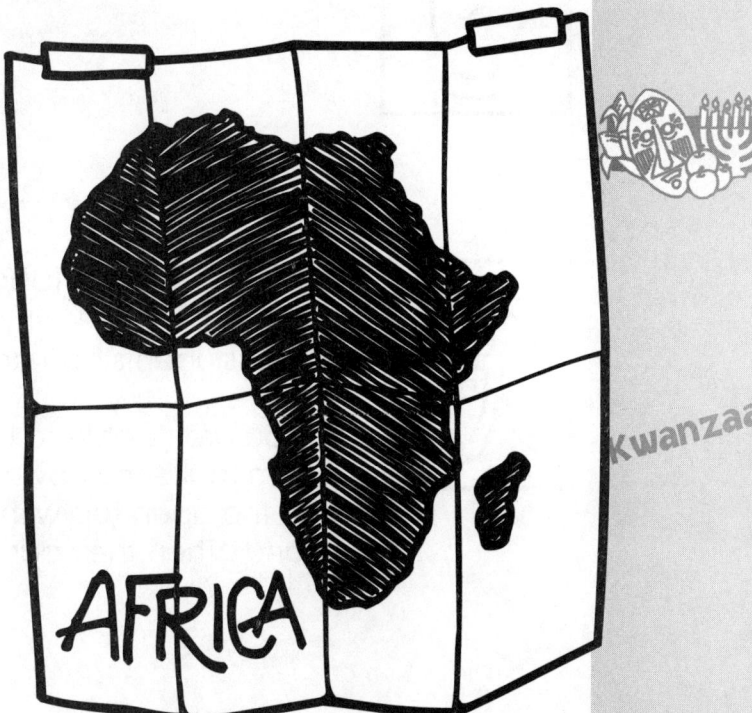

Music/Dramatic Experience

- Borrow African drums for students to beat in time to an African music recording from your local library.

Physical/Sensory Experience

- Let students dance to African music, making up their own dance steps.

Arts/Crafts Experience

- Browse through Kathy Ross' *Crafts for Kwanzaa* for some craft activity ideas students can do today.

- If you aren't able to borrow African drums for students to play, let them make their own drums by painting round oatmeal boxes, covering the open top with plastic or oil cloth and securing it with a rubber band. Then they can play their drums.

Quilt-Mania Day

December 27

Setting the Stage

- Display quilts around related literature to gather excitement in the day's emphasis.
- Construct a semantic web with facts your students know (or would like to know) about quilts.

Historical Background

Throughout history quilts have been a part of our culture. They are works of art that often tell stories and preserve memories through creative designs and patterns. December is a good time of year to snuggle up with a warm quilt and dream happy dreams.

Literary Exploration

Before I Was Born by Harriet Ziefert
Bizzy Bones and the Lost Quilt by Jacqueline Martin
The Boy and the Quilt by Shirley Kurtz
The Canada Geese Quilt by Natalie Kinsey-Warnock
Cinnamon Bear: The Missing Star by Glan and Elisabeth Heisch
The Crazy Quilt by Kristin Avery
Eight Hands Round: A Patchwork Alphabet by Ann Whitford Paul
Ernest and Celestine's Patchwork Quilt by Gabrielle Vincent
The Josefina Story Quilt by Eleanor Coerr
The Keeping Quilt by Patricia Polacco
Luka's Quilt by Georgia Guback
The Patchwork Lady by Mary K. Whittington
The Patchwork Quilt by Valerie Flournoy
Patchwork Tales by Susan L. Roth
The Quilt by Ann Jonas
The Quilt Story by Tony Johnston
Sam Johnson and the Blue Ribbon Quilt by Lisa Campbell Ernst
Selina and the Bear Paw Quilt by Barbara Smucker
Sweet Clara and the Freedom Quilt by Deborah Hopkinson

Language Experience

- Create a class Venn diagram depicting the similarities and differences between a blanket and a quilt.

Writing Experience

- If you have access to a quilt with various pictures in each quilt block, display it. Let each student choose a block to write a story about.

Math Experience

- The squares on a quilt make a good framework for an addition or multiplication table chart.

Arts/Crafts Experience

- Provide each student with a small sheet of art paper like a quilt square. Let them decorate their squares any way they want. Then bring all the pieces together and staple them to form a class paper quilt that can be mounted or displayed on a bulletin board.

Extension Activities

⚠ Create an Edible Quilt together. Bake a cake, then draw narrow lines on it with squeeze-tube frosting to look like quilt squares. Students can decorate individual squares with their initials, using candies, raisins or nuts. Then eat the quilt!

- Try making a class quilt. Give each student a 6-inch square of cotton or muslin and some fabric markers. After they decorate their squares, iron over the designs, putting a couple pieces of paper between. The color will set. Decide on the quilt layout, then let parent volunteers sew the squares and assemble the quilt. Display the class quilt on a wooden dowel for all to enjoy.

Woodrow Wilson's Birthday

December 28

Setting the Stage
- Construct a semantic web with facts your students know (or would like to know) about Woodrow Wilson.

Historical Background
Woodrow Wilson, the 28th President of the United States, was born on this day in 1856.

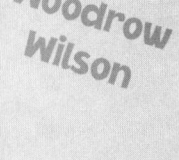

Literary Exploration
Woodrow Wilson by Perry Leavell
Woodrow Wilson by Alice Osinski
Woodrow Wilson: Boy President by Helen Albee Monsell
Woodrow Wilson: 28th President of the United States by David R. Collins
The Woodrow Wilson Story by Catherine Peare

Language Experience
- Ask students what words they think of when they hear the word *peace*. Write their ideas on the board.

- Woodrow Wilson was known as a "crusader" for peace. Challenge students to find out what that word means.

Writing Experience
- Woodrow Wilson spent much of his political career promoting world peace. He was awarded the Nobel Peace Prize in 1920. Have students write about what they would like to see world leaders do to promote peaceful resolutions between warring countries. See reproducible on page 171.

Social Studies Experience

- As a class, learn about Woodrow Wilson's life and presidency.

- Let interested students do additional research on the years of World War I, then share their findings with the rest of the class.

- Wilson became President in 1913 and served two terms. Challenge students to find out which Presidents served immediately before him and just after him (Taft and Harding).

- Wilson was born in Virginia. Have students point out Virginia on a United States map. He was elected president of Princeton University in New Jersey in 1902. Have them locate New Jersey on the map. Wilson left the school in 1910 when he became governor of New Jersey.

Arts/Crafts Experience

- Woodrow Wilson was tall and slender, often with a serious look on his face. He wore rimless glasses and was almost always dressed in a suit and tie. After sharing this description with the students, have them draw portraits of President Woodrow Wilson.

Values Education Experience

- President Wilson never gave up trying to be a peacemaker in the world. Discuss the need for peacemakers. Ask students to share their ideas for making and keeping peace between schoolmates, family and all those with whom they come in contact. Write their peace-making ideas on the board and discuss them.

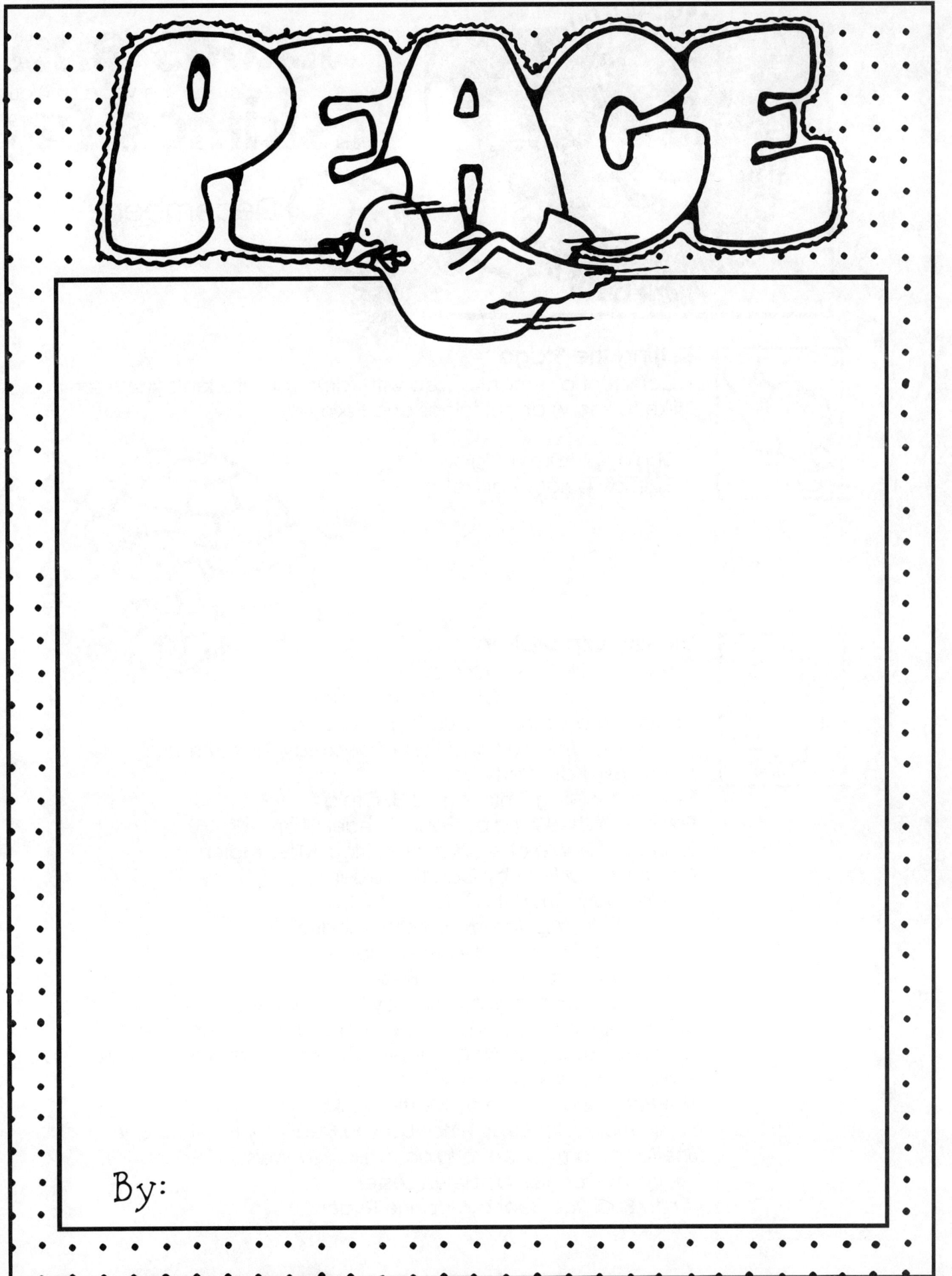

Igloos and Eskimos Day

December 29

Setting the Stage

- Construct a semantic web with facts your students know (or would like to know) about igloos and Eskimos.

- Display pictures of igloos, Eskimos, polar bears, etc.

Literary Exploration

Antarctica by Helen Cowcher
A Child's Alaska by Claire Rudolf Murphy
Dance on a Sealskin by Barbara Winslow
The Eskimo: The Inuit and Yupik People by Alice Osinski
Eskimos by Kate Petty
Eskimos by Greg Smith and J.H. Greig
Eskimos of the World by Paul Michael Elliott
Eskimos: People of Alaska by Patricai Miles Martin
Great Crystal Bear by Carolyn Lesser
The Igloo by Charlotte Yue
Igloos, Yurts, and Totem Poles by Friedrich Boer
King Island Christmas by Jean Rogers
Little Polar Bear by Hans de Beer
Little Polar Bear Finds a Friend by Hans DeBeer
Mr. Popper's Penguins by Richard and Florence Atwater
Northern Lullaby by Nancy White Carlstrom and Leo and Diane Dillon
Polar Bear Cubs by Downs Matthews
The Polar Bear on Ice by Martin Banks
Polar Bear, Polar Bear, What Do You Hear? by Bill Martin, Jr.
Shelters: From Tepee to Igloo by Harvey Weiss
Tacky the Penguin by Helen Lester
White Bear, Ice Bear by Joanne Ryder

Language Experience
- Let your students brainstorm other words that have the "oo" sound as in *igloo*.

Writing Experience

- Let student write stories about an Eskimo child who moves to Florida. What is different? What does the child like and dislike? Have them use the reproducible on page 176.

- Have students imagine they live in an igloo. Let them describe their lives in such a unique house.

What I like and dislike about *my new home.*

Science/Health Experience

- Learn about penguins and other polar animals. How are their bodies different from other birds and mammals to adapt to the cold climate? See reproducible on page 177.

Arctic Animals

LC10465 Copyright © Teaching & Learning Company, Carthage, IL 62321-0010

Social Studies Experience

- Learn about the Eskimo people and their way of life.

- Some Inuit people rub noses instead of shaking hands when they meet. Ask students how they would like that. When would they not like it. Let a few friends of the same gender try it.

Physical/Sensory Experience

- Eskimo children make string designs such as the familiar "Cat's Cradle" from animal sinew. For yarn and string game ideas for your students to try, check out Caroline Jayne's book, *String Figures and How to Make Them*.

Arts/Crafts Experience

- Make igloos out of sugar cubes or marshmallows stuck together with peanut butter around a cored apple half.

- Students can make fuzzy polar bears by gluing cotton balls on for a three-dimensional effect. See reproducible on page 178.

Extension Activities

⚠ Make Edible Polar Bears. Students can dip a large marshmallow in melted chocolate chips, then roll it in shredded coconut for a yummy treat!

⚠ Serve the ice cream treat, Eskimo Pies™!

Moving!

What I like and dislike about my new home.

Arctic Animals

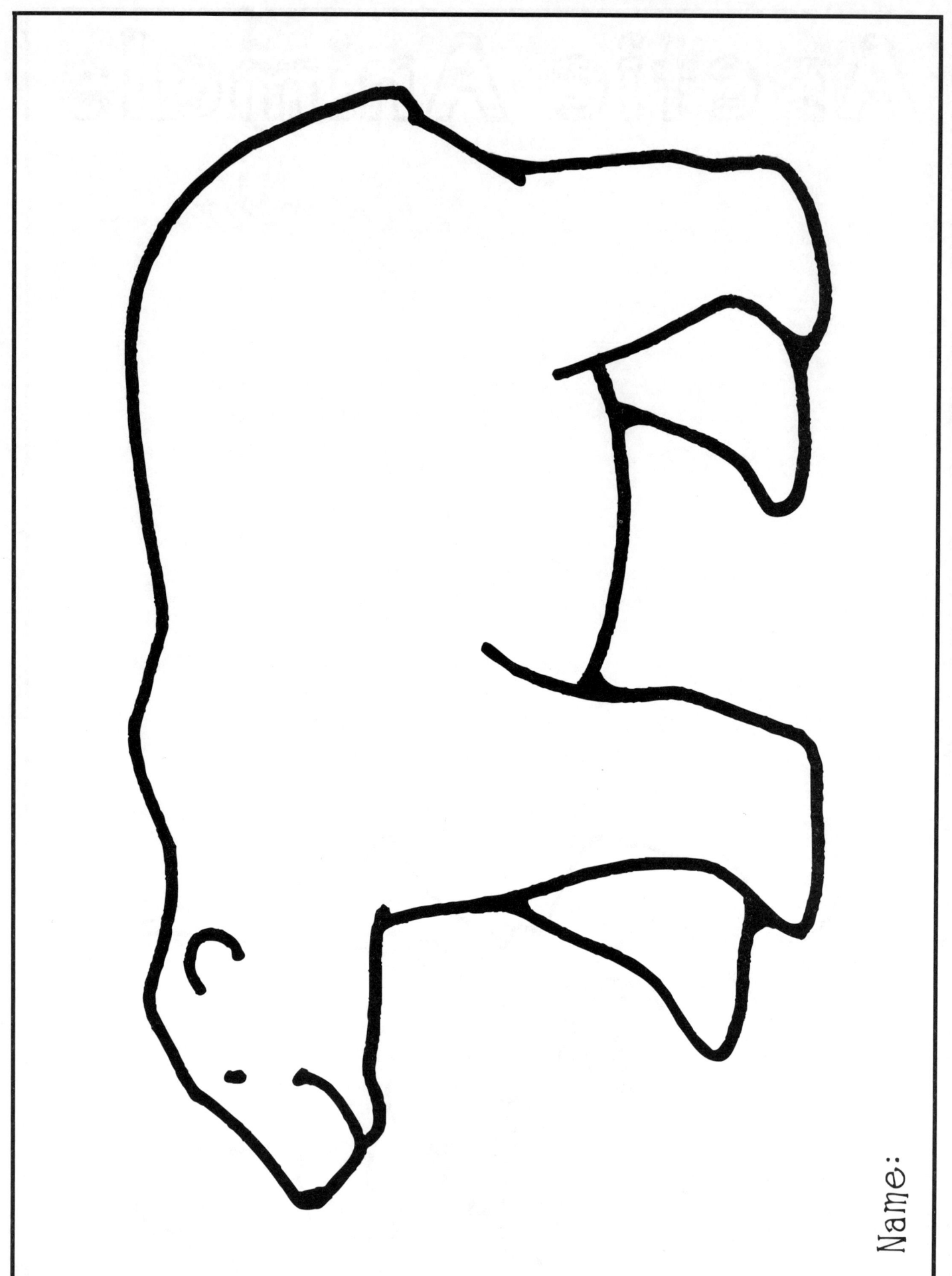

Rudyard Kipling's Birthday

December 30

Setting the Stage
- Construct a semantic web with facts your students know (or would like to know) about Rudyard Kipling.

Historical Background
The British writer, Rudyard Kipling, was born on this day in 1865. He is famous for his *Just So Stories* and *The Jungle Book*.

Literary Exploration
The Jungle Book by Rudyard Kipling
Just So Stories by Rudyard Kipling
Kipling: Storyteller of East and West by Gloria Kamen
Rudyard Kipling: Author of the Jungle Books by Carol Greene

Language Experience
- Rudyard Kipling was a writer of both prose and poetry. Read one of his poems aloud, then say a word and have students think of all the words they can that rhyme with it. Continue with other words and rhymes.

Writing Experience
- Rudyard Kipling won the Nobel Prize in the literature category in 1907. After reading some of his *Just So Stories,* have students write their own "Just So Stories." (Example: "How the Raccoon Got His Mask") Hand out Nobel Prizes to the authors. See reproducibles on page 182.

- Have interested students do additional research to discover what Kipling won the Nobel Prize for. They can share what they learn with the class.

Social Studies Experience

- Rudyard Kipling spent many years in India. Have students find India on a map. He wrote stories about the animals he saw there: tigers, elephants, snakes and others. *The Jungle Book* takes place in India.

- Have students research some of the animals Kipling wrote about to find out their habitat, the food they eat and if they are dangerous to people. Let them share their findings with one another.

Physical/Sensory Experience

- Let students take turns pantomiming animals in Kipling's books while the rest of the class tries to guess what they are.

Arts/Crafts Experience

- Let students illustrate one of Rudyard Kipling's *Just So Stories* or one of their own.

- Mount a long strip of shelf paper on a wall and let students work together to draw a jungle mural as they imagine it from *The Jungle Book*.

Extension Activities

⚠ Invite grandparents to visit your class and watch *The Jungle Book* movie with their grandchildren (your students). Serve popcorn while everyone enjoys the story.

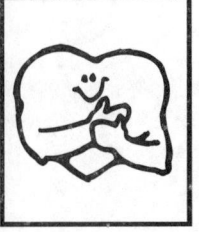

Values Education Experience

- After reading *The Jungle Book* or watching the movie, ask students what positive character traits Mowgli had. How did those help him survive life in the jungle and escape from danger? Ask students to consider if they are like Mowgli in any of these ways.

182

New Year's Eve Day

December 31

Setting the Stage
- Construct a semantic web with facts your students know (or would like to know) about New Year's Eve celebrations.

Historical Background
December 31st is the day before the first day of the New Year. There are countdown activities until midnight, then fireworks are set off, noisemakers are played and people welcome in a new year with fun.

Literary Exploration
Christmastime in New York City by Roxie Munro
Happy New Year! by Emily Kelley
Miss Flora McFlimsey and the Baby New Year by Mariana

Language Experience
- Have students share New Year's Eve customs and traditions in their families.

- Challenge students to think of New Year's resolutions they want to make. Discuss the word *resolution*. Ask them to tell what they think it means.

Writing Experience

- Have students reflect upon the past year and write about some of their memories. See reproducible on page 186.

- Let students think what other people (neighbors, a teacher or friend) might do for New Year's Eve. They can even think about a famous person if they want. Have them write about what the people might do.

Social Studies Experience

- Research New Year's Eve festivities around the world. How did they begin? How are they different from one another? How are they the same?

Physical/Sensory Experience

- Bring store-bought or hand-made noisemakers (musical instruments, pots and pans, pie-tin tambourines) to class. Have an early New Year's Eve celebration. (Warn neighboring classes what you're going to do.)

Arts/Crafts Experience

- Students can make their own "noisemakers." They cut out a paper strip about four inches long and fold it down the middle. They cut one end and fold it back each by one inch. They hold the straight ends together and fold the two bent ends in a "T" shape. To make a sound, the student holds the base of the "T" between the second and third fingers (with the palm facing them). They blow against the top of the "T" shape. Presto! Instant noisemaker! See the reproducibles on page 187.

- Let students make New Year's hats! They form a cone shape from construction paper and glue on glitter, sequins, buttons, bows, etc. for a zany hat. A cluster of yarn can be a "tassel."

Extension Activities

- Students will enjoy making a class time capsule. Have them brainstorm and collect items that seem to typify the year going out. Store them in a shoe box and hide it until the end of the school year. (Be sure to note where it is hidden and when to bring it out so it can be shared at the appropriate time.)

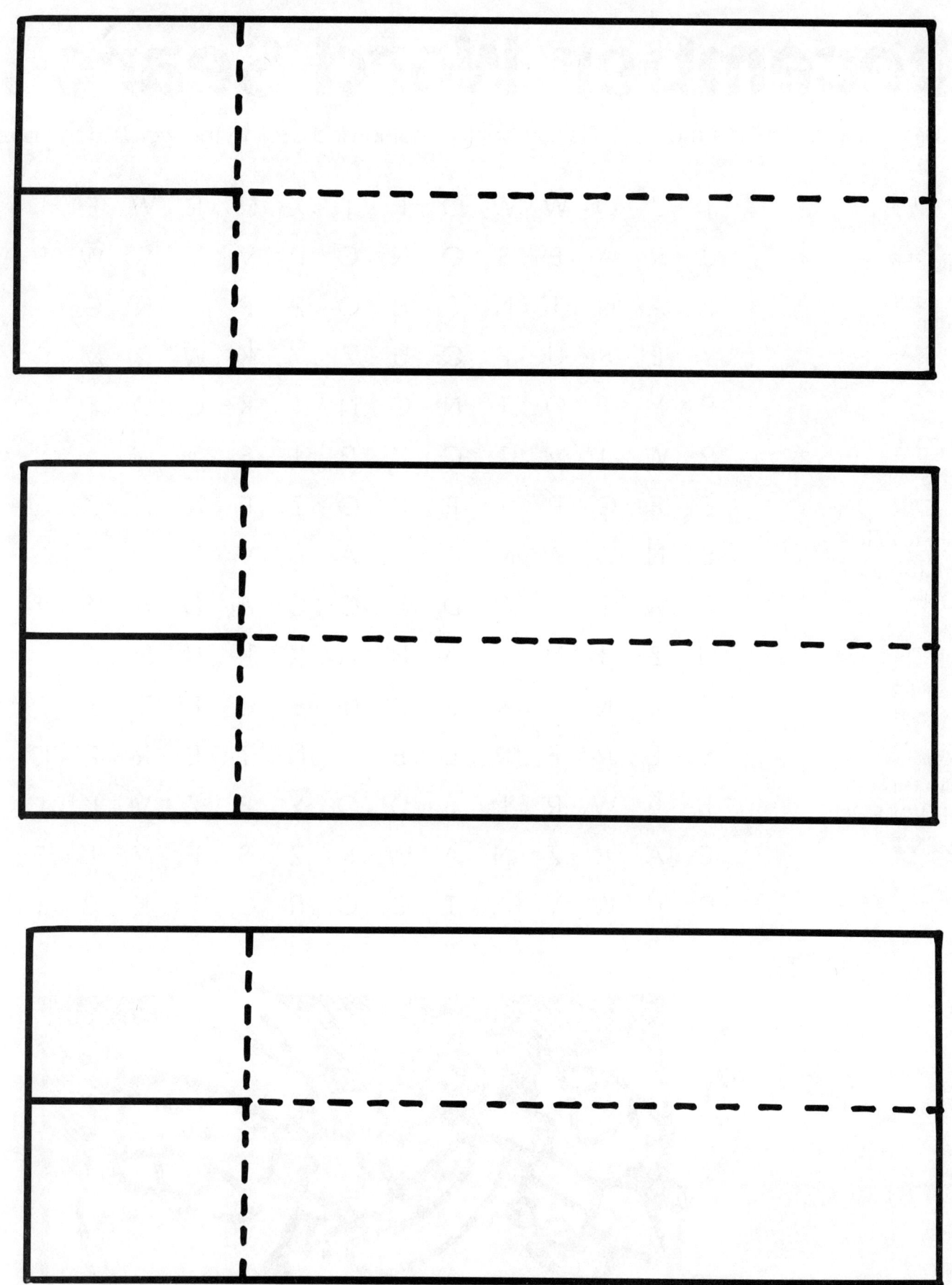

December Word Search

Celebrate and review the month of December by finding and circling the words in the puzzle.

- CHRISTMAS
- COLD
- DECEMBER
- ELVES
- FROZEN
- HANUKKAH
- HAT
- ICE
- KWANZAA
- MITTENS
- NEW YEAR
- NUTCRACKER
- PRESENTS
- REINDEER
- SANTA
- SCARF
- SHOPPING
- SLED
- SNOW
- SNOWMAN
- SOUTH POLE
- STOCKING
- TREE
- WINTER

```
I J O W Q F I X M R W E F I
S R A E S O N C R V Y C W R R
L A N I N S H O P P I N G A S
Y E S U E Q U Z Y K W R M C H
P Y T O T N G N I K C O T S I
R W J M T C H R I S T M A S N
E E G P I F R O Z E N N K O H
S N O W M A N A H V T O R U L
E W T I C D L O C A Q A W T V
N Z J N T A H A K K U N A H M
T L K T R E B M E C E D A P L
S L R E R E E D N I E R R O S
L E W R L L D Q Y B Z V K L F
E A A Z N A W K Z S E V L E C
D U W Y A T O C R O F K P T B
```

December Word Scramble

Draw a line from each scrambled word on the right to the way it should look on the left.

CHRISTMAS	CEBEERDM
COLD	YENWEAR
DECEMBER	SEEVL
ELVES	NWOS
FROZEN	SDEL
HANUKKAH	OZNFRE
HAT	RCASF
ICE	INEDREER
KWANZAA	SEENTSRP
MITTENS	OCDL
NEW YEAR	ERET
NUTCRACKER	AKWAZAN
PRESENTS	THA
REINDEER	NIWTRE
SANTA	POSIHNGP
SCARF	MAWNOSN
SHOPPING	CERCKAUTNR
SLED	UOPLESHTO
SNOW	KAHUNKAH
SNOWMAN	ECI
SOUTH POLE	MTSCHRAIS
STOCKING	ITENSMT
TREE	OKSCINTG
WINTER	ASTAN

189

How many new words can you make using the letters in December Snow?

_____   _____
_____   _____
_____   _____
_____   _____
_____   _____
_____   _____
_____   _____

Answer Key for page 139

State the State Crossword Puzzle

Across
1. Wisconsin
4. Washington
8. Texas
9. Illinois

Down
2. Oregon
3. Nevada
5. Alaska
6. Indiana
7. New York
10. Ohio

Cross-Number Puzzle

Across
3. 24
4. 1602
5. 44
6. 2001
7. 240

Downs
1. 365
2. 222
3. 24
5. 412

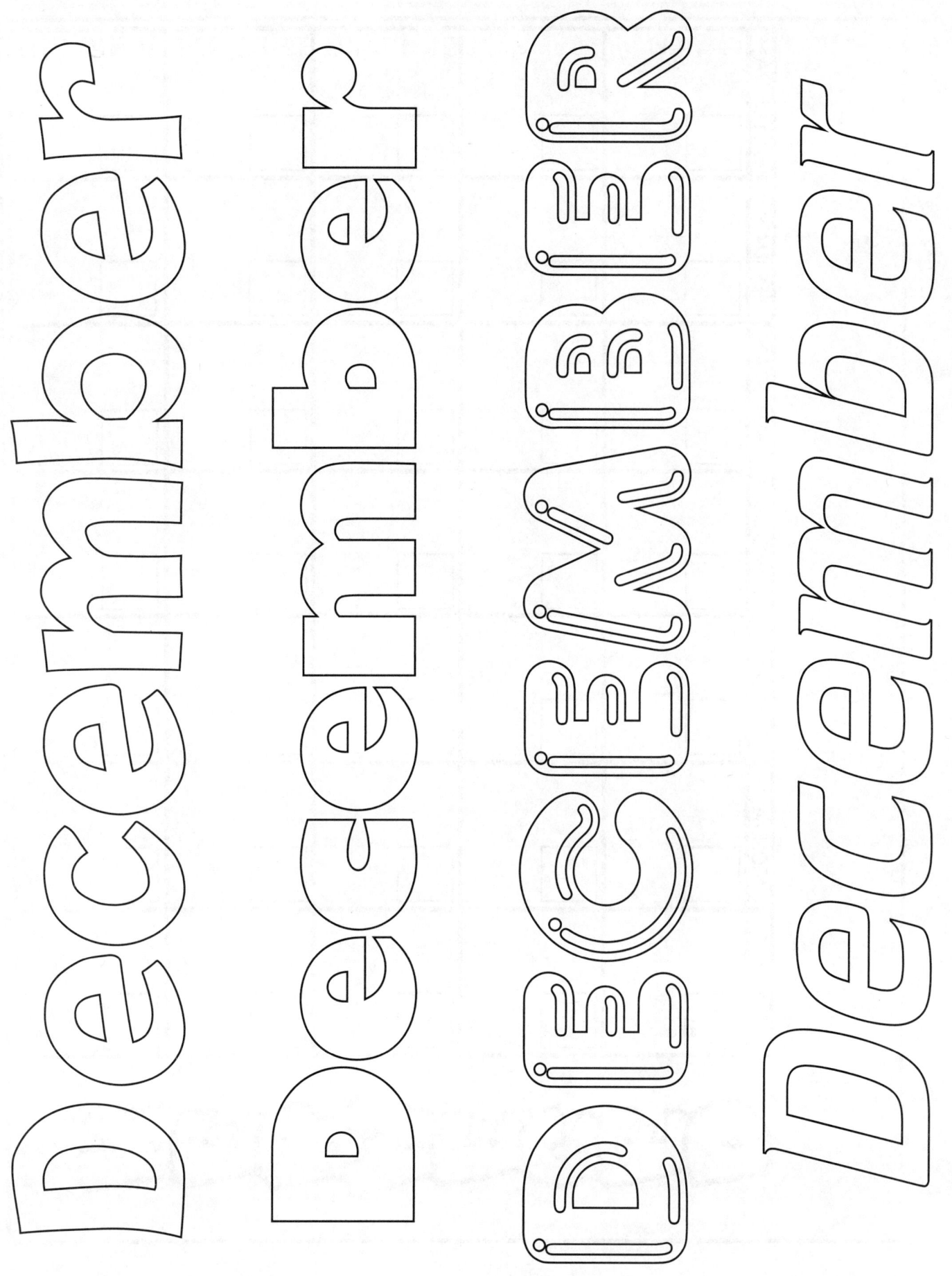

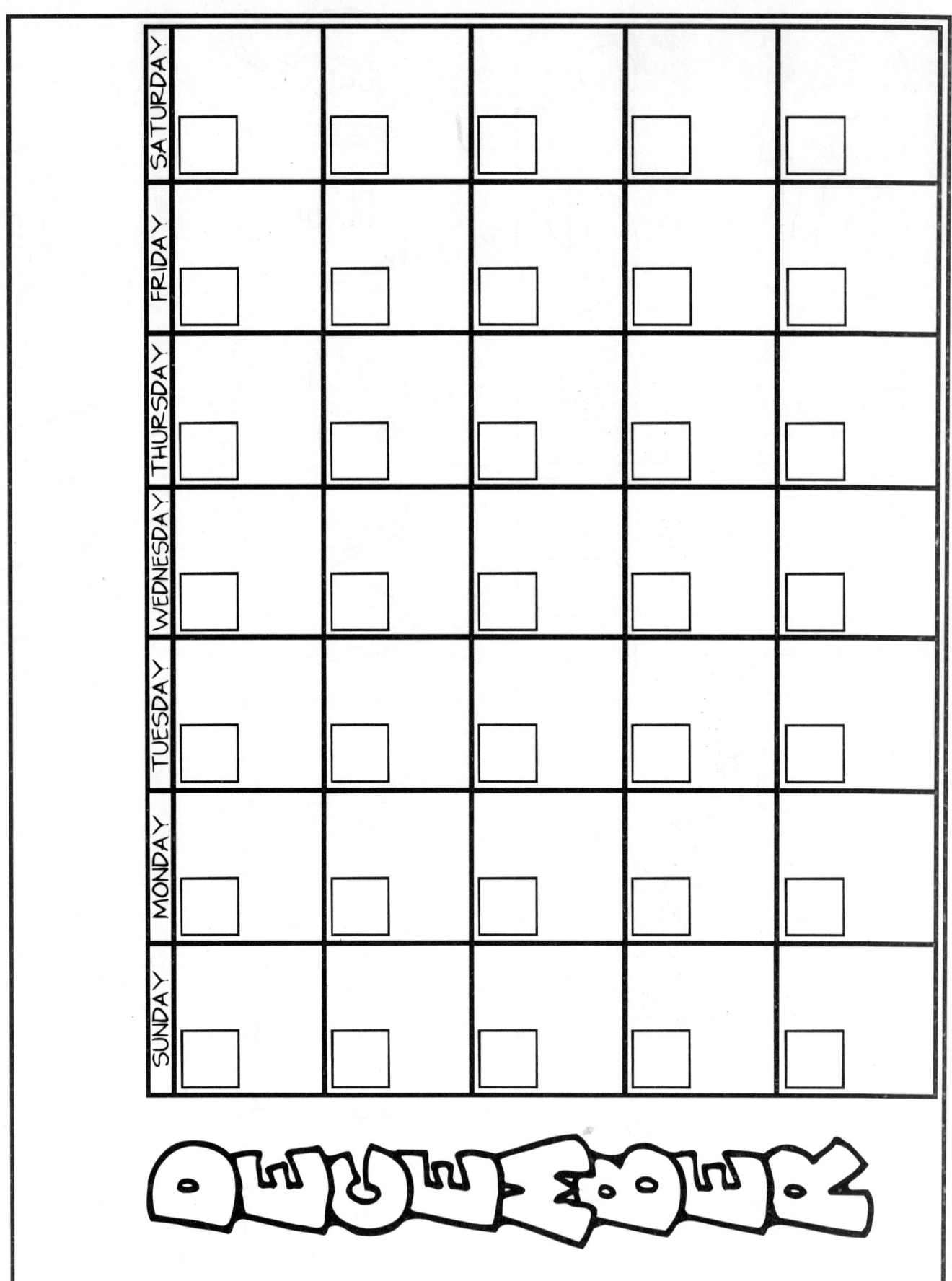